The Step-By-Step Guide To Blogging

By Pat Marcello

Edited by Tellman Knudson, CEO
Overcome Everything, Inc.

Introduction

Inside this book you're going to learn how a multi-million dollar company does blogging on the internet.

And the truth is, it's no different than anyone else doing it the right way. Yes, there is a right way and a very WRONG way. A blog can be the most powerful communications asset and lead generation tool you can have, when you do it the right way. It isn't hard, but it does require a little patience and persistence. This book contains everything you'll need to know, the tools and resources you'll want to have at your disposal, and guided illustrations to hold your hand every step of the way.

Once you've got the right tools, all that's left is to develop a few easy habits. That's where the success comes from -- the habits. For someone who loves to write, blogging can be the most rewarding thing you can do, both personally and professionally.

Just imagine… Once you learn these few easy steps, you can express your passions, hobbies, poetry… whatever inspires and motivates you… you'll be able to instantly share it with others in written word, spoken and recorded, or even caught on video.

Getting readers and subscribers, and turning them into paying customers is also free. Selling advertising space on your blog (once you've got a few regular eyeballs on your page) is also 100% free. Promoting affiliate programs, products and services to your growing readership.

And if you are willing to spend a little cash, you can actually get other qualified bloggers to do most of the work for you!

Your profit margins could not be better. All you need to know is already inside this book. So, take the time and effort to go through each and every step. Follow along closely, and perform each action item as it is given inside each Chapter. By the time you've finished the book, you'll have a killer blog already set up and getting subscribers!

Keep repeating these easy steps, and your personal income will increase, as your readership and subscriber count get bigger. This really is the secret to big success with blogging.

And it all begins here...

WHY IS BLOGGING IMPORTANT?

Blogging is a very important activity if you want to do business online. The WordPress platform is so flexible and customizable that you can set up any type of website you want. But, you may wonder what makes blogging so special…

First, blogs are an excellent way to bond with the people in your niche. People will read a blog with helpful information to solve problems they're having or to make whatever they're doing better. This is a wonderful way to get people to know, like, and *trust* you. Without trust, you won't be able to sell anything online.

Second, blogs are search engine friendly. Search engines love nothing more than fresh content. Blogs are updated much more often than standard websites. Plus, blogs come with a feature that makes the material on your blog easy to read called an RSS feed. This feed contains nothing but pure text from the posts that you make to your blog. There are no pictures, no JavaScript, or anything that might slow search engine spiders (robots that automatically search the web for new information) down.

This adaptability of WordPress, and the inherent RSS feed makes it the darling of search. If you're posting in your blog regularly and using appropriate keywords for your niche, you will be showing up regularly the search engine results pages. A first-place listing at Google for a keyword people are actively searching for is your ticket to targeted, organic (natural) free traffic, which is, of course, the best kind.

HOW CAN A BLOG HELP TO BUILD MY LIST?

Once you have people interested in what you have to say, blogging is also an extremely powerful way to build your list. From reading your blog, your potential customer already knows you. If your presentation helps them to like and trust you, they'll be much more inclined to sign up for your list than the list of someone they don't know at all.

There are a couple of ways to set up lead generation systems with your blog, which we'll cover in this book, very powerful ways that can give you a high optin rate and lots of happy subscribers.

What I want you to accomplish

I'm writing this book with goals in mind. Without a solid goal for you to achieve, you probably won't make much progress. Seeing your results improve and knowing the path you need to follow are two very important aspects of a successful training program.

However, we cannot guarantee your results unless YOU take action, and complete the activities in this book to the letter. Nothing happens until you decide to commit to this system, and if you don't commit your time, energy, and money to it, you probably won't get the same results.

AND, you must USE the resources we have laid out for you. If you choose other resources for your autoresponder and hosting, for example, we cannot assure you that the system will work as it's been proven to do. You can't bake a cake substituting baking soda for baking powder, for example, or you'll have a very flat cake.

With those things said, here are the things you should be able to achieve by reading the book and following each lesson as it's laid out for you. I want you to:

- Get your first blog up and running
- Get a reliable and reasonably priced hosting account
- Buy your first domain
- Set up your first squeeze page
- Be able to drive traffic to your squeeze page
- To get at least 100 optins to your subscriber list
- To make your first dollar online

Those are very reachable goals if you simply follow the system we have laid out for you.

WHY IS THIS IMPORTANT?

Following our system to the letter is very important, not to us, but to your ultimate success. Here are some other reasons:

- We want you to see that making money online is very doable. Achieving the goals we've set forth above will let you see that you can do it!
- We want you to have a sense of accomplishment
- We want you to be writing to your specific audience and be creating content for your readers

All of these reasons are important to keeping you interested in what you're doing and to show you that it can be done. Getting your feet wet and making your first dollar will give you the needed enthusiasm to keep you going, day after day.

HOW LONG WILL IT TAKE?

If you start today, you can go through materials and if you follow step-by-step, it's possible to have everything set up and running in the next 30 days. But that means you need to spend time with building your system on a routine schedule. Get into the habit of working on your business for a **set** amount of time each and every day.

Start by setting aside one hour a day to work on your online business. Even if you're just reading, make sure to dedicate that hour to your business, not surfing the Web, not sending tweets out on Twitter, but working toward setting up your business *system*. If you can afford two hours or more, all the better, but be sure that you set a *routine*.

For example, if you can work on your business 8 hours a day, 5 days a week, just as if you had a job, this is optimal. But I encourage you to keep your day job if online marketing is new to you. You will need a regular income to sustain you while you're building a new business.

If you're new to computers, our 30-day plan may also take longer than if you're up to speed with the technology. That's OK… Follow your routine, and you'll accomplish the same thing as people who are already tech savvy. It may just take slightly longer.

You need to develop a new HABIT. That's the key. Although you might be a person who enjoys the online marketing atmosphere, there will be days that you don't feel like messing with it. THOSE are the days when having a routine – a habit—will come in handy. You can't allow yourself to step on your own foot.

Developing the habit will probably take about two weeks. The best way to establish it is to work on your business at the same TIME every day, for the same length of time. So, don't be erratic. Stick to a schedule as closely as you possibly can.

I have to tell you, though, that many of my students have had enormous success with their online businesses, and I have noticed that speed played a major part in their success. So, do as much as you can in your allotted time and don't allow anything to distract you.

The sad thing is that many of you aren't motivated to do anything. You may not ever read this book! You'll buy it, put it on your shelf, and that will be that. But for those of you who have that goal we discussed above set for yourself and who can stay motivated, even when you're not seeing outrageous results immediately, you'll do very well if you just follow your ROUTINE.

WHAT KEEPS YOU UP AT NIGHT?

If you bought this book and are a complete techno-phobe, forget that! We're going to show you how to do everything you need to do in easy-to-understand chapters to move you forward.

Remember something: You can't BREAK the Internet! It's not possible. You WILL make mistakes. I made plenty of them starting out, and you will, too. But all mistakes are correctable, overall, and if you're going through the lessons and doing what we tell you to do, your chances of success are automatically much stronger.

So, from the goals that we have set down for you, create baby steps that you can achieve easily and give you a better sense of accomplishment. For example, we want you to get your first blog installed. A baby steps goal could be logging into cPanel in your hosting account for the first time. The second step would be locating Fantastico, and the third step, installing your blog. Breaking bigger goals into smaller chunks are very helpful in giving you a sense of accomplishment.

WHAT GREAT NEW THING WILL COMPLETING OUR PROGRAM DO FOR YOU?

If you're interested in earning extra money, having this system set up will undoubtedly provide a second income stream for you. It may not be enough to help you quit your job at first, but as your list grows, so will your income and your influence in your niche.

Once you have this system and our other Step-by-Step Guide systems completed, you will have more control over your time. You will be able to reach the goal of quitting your job, for example. You'll be able to work less, and you will ultimately be able to make more money than you're making now.

The ultimate benefit of working through our Step-by-Step guides will be freedom. You will be able to work where ever you want to work and to do whatever you want to do, every single day. Who doesn't want to sit on a beach with their laptop computer, send an email, and earn enough to stay on vacation for another day? This is totally doable, and much, much more.

The days of worrying about how you will pay the bills, send your kids to college, or reaching your life's goal of traveling the globe will be over! With our Step-by-Step guides, if you follow them, and set them up the way we instruct you to do, anything will be possible!

You'll be able to help other people, too. Imagine having the money to help your parents or kids buy new houses. Or what about sending your wonder student to an Ivy League school, paying off your uncle's hospital bill, or giving the money you earn to your favorite charity?

Having this type of income from your online business is completely doable. I know because I've done it. My company, Overcome Everything, Inc., is now a multi-million dollar company, though I started out with $50 and a broken-down computer. I'm absolute proof that this type of freedom and income can be achieved.

And I have taught thousands of people to do the same thing. My students have made millions of dollars on their own from the training that I have given them. It works!

Help yourself by letting it work for you! Make the commitment right now to follow along with this book, and to DO what the book tells you to do. For much of what you'll learn in here, we have videos online that will help you to see what needs doing and how to do it right before your eyes.

So, that's it! Don't listen to your friends and relatives who want to tell you you'll never make a dime online. They're wrong!

They have no experience with what you're doing, and… if you commit, if you set your goals wisely, and if you follow these lessons to the letter – you can laugh all the way to the bank.

SHABAMBO!

- Tellman Knudson, Editor and CEO of Overcome Everything, Inc.

CHAPTER ONE:

CHOOSING THE RIGHT NICHE FOR YOU

Before you even decide on what your platform's going to be, what your business is going to be, you really need to start thinking about where you want to start your business. In other words, what niche do you want to market products in?

This is a hard thing for a lot of people to nail down. They're just so nervous that they're going to pick the wrong thing, or they don't think that they'll make any money with what it is, you know, what they're thinking about doing, and so on. But, you know, I think that we have been over and over and over it again with List Building Club members and with a lot of different people about how to pick a niche.

For most people getting started online, a common question we hear is, "Well, how do I make money online? What product do I sell?" And that's really the wrong way to start. Most people try to start with a product, or a good idea, or a new idea, and you really want to start with a specific niche market. So what's really cool about that is once you decide what market you want to go into, there is an endless amount of products that you could create yourself or promote as an affiliate.

> *Tip: Think about what you already love or want to learn more about before picking your niche*

So, if you're sitting around all day thinking, *Well, what product should I sell?* That's a really tough question to answer because there are hundreds, and millions of different products out there, right? There are products for everything. If you start with the market, and you say, "Well, I want to be in the self-improvement market, or I want to be in the weight loss market," or whatever market you go into, once you say, "Well, I'm in the weight loss market,"– the answer to that question is easy. "What should I sell?" "Well, I should sell products that help people lose weight," or "I should sell products that help people do whatever they need to do, or solve whatever problem they are in the market area."

The first thing I would do is take an inventory of all of my passions and interests because you absolutely have to enjoy what you do, and have a passion for what you're doing, otherwise it's just going to seem like another job. And who wants that, right?

A Common Mistake

One common thing that people do, which is probably the absolute wrong thing to do, is to jump into the "make money" niche. The best reason for that is that they haven't made any money online yet, so how can they teach other people how to do it, or to be successful in teaching other people how to do it.

They don't know the difference between a good product and a bad product when it comes to other people's training on how to make money online, either. Plus, it's so competitive! There are hundreds of know marketing "gurus," and they have big companies behind them -- big systems behind them -- and they're making tons of money because they got to the trough first.

Some of the biggest names in the Internet marketing world have been around for a very long time. They have huge lists of subscribers that know their names and trust them for the quality of information they bring to the table. Their subscribers have used their trainings, and know that what they teach works. They have reputation and history behind them. But if you're just starting out, it's really not possible to teach people what you don't know much about yourself.

They learned it, and they know what they're doing.

So a really big mistake is for people to just jump right in and think that they can get into the make money niche and become a millionaire overnight. Some people have, it's true. Some people are that adept technically, already know something about marketing, and they can get a system together and make it work for them. I'm not saying nobody can do it, ever, but that's where most people think they need to go, and that's absolutely not true. In fact, it's just the opposite. They'll have faster and better success if they find a niche that works well for them, personally.

Tip: You can find the Google keyword tool at https://adwords.google.com/o/Targeting/Explorer

Pick something that you're passionate about, but it definitely helps if it's something that you already have knowledge about because it just makes your job so much easier. You're already facing some challenges going into business; you have to learn all the techniques, all the technology. You have to learn the marketing, and there are several different skill sets you have to develop to have a successful online business. Why add the challenge to that of actually having to learn the material that's relevant to the business you're in from scratch?

For example, let's talk about the fitness niche. Say you already workout a lot, you know everything there is to know about diet, nutrition, and it's something you're passionate about, that's a really great market to go into, and having that knowledge helps because you already know the problems and the challenges that the market faces. You know what the solutions are. You have experience with that market. You can develop your own opinions on that market. And you have a lot to bring to the table.

If you don't know anything about the market, that's just going to make your job a million times harder, and if you've never made money online -- what gives you the right to teach other people to make money online? That just doesn't make sense.

But getting back to your passion -- what you're good at, what you already know about. In fact, there are many things that you know about that you don't even consider for your business.
For example, a lot of people love gardening. There's a good niche. A lot of people like working out and training and exercise, and there are all kinds of things that you probably know about already that would make it really so much easier for you. But you really need to think about whether or not it's going to be profitable.

Will the Niche I Choose Make Money?

This is a prime consideration when picking a niche. If nobody is searching for the keywords that surround your niche, you probably won't do very well. You want to see that at least 10,000 people a month have some interest in what it is you want to sell.

Go to Goggle, use their AdWords external keyword tool and plug in some really general terms for your niche. If you want to go into the golfing niche, or whatever niche it might be, just plug it into Goggle and see what pops up.

For example, you may plug in "golf." Here are some of the terms that show up:

Keyword	Competition	Global Monthly Searches
golf		37,200,000
golf club		3,350,000
golf equipment		1,220,000
golf clubs		1,000,000
golf courses		823,000
mini golf		550,000
callaway golf		246,000
golf games		165,000
pga golf		110,000
golf club sets		74,000
second hand golf clubs		74,000
used golf clubs		60,500

Obviously, with 37 million people searching for golf, you've got a good niche. Yet, just being in the "golf" niche is a little too general. The more you can narrow your search, the better. For example, move down the list and you'll see: golf equipment, used golf clubs, and golf club reviews. Any of those would make stellar niches, but there are many more options.

On the other hand, what if you're interested in selling lawn darts? Here's what we see in the chart below:

Keyword	Searches
unicorn darts	9,900
plant games	8,100
lawn games	8,100
darts rules	8,100
backyard games	8,100
yard games	6,600
lawn darts	6,600
outdoor party games	6,600
fun outdoor games	6,600

We didn't even start at the top of the list in this case because so many terms came back, but notice something important: "lawn darts" gets a mere 6,600 searches a month globally. That's really not enough interest to build a business around. However, not all is lost.

But go ahead and do the search in Google. Notice that further up the list, above 10,000 searches per month, you can see "outside games" and "darts games," both of which could include "lawn darts," so in that case, if you just got a little more *general*, you'd have a pretty good niche.

But some niches just aren't at all viable. A search for "chipmunk coats" will come back with lots of terms about coats and types of coats, but if you're intending to sew coats for chipmunks, though it's a little silly, it's very obviously NOT a niche you want to get into.

You have to do a little research to **make sure that you are in a niche that people are actually searching for and buying products in**. One of the most common objections I hear is when someone says – well, they've identified their passion is, they say, "Well, someone's already doing it though." So someone might say, "Well, yeah, I am passionate about fitness," or "I am passionate about golf," or "I am passionate about coin collecting," or whatever it is. And they say, "But there's already people out there doing it."

You have to do a little research to **make sure that you are in a niche that people are actually searching for and buying products in**. One of the most common objections I hear is when someone says – well, they've identified their passion is, they say, "Well, someone's already doing it though." So someone might say, "Well, yeah, I am passionate about fitness," or "I am passionate about golf," or "I am passionate about coin collecting," or whatever it is. And they say, "But there's already people out there doing it."

> *Tip: "If you go into a market with no competition, there's probably no competition because there's no money being made"*

And a lot of people get scared of competition, but really, I say that you really should **go into a competitive markets because competitive markets is where the money is**, so we know what a lot of these big markets are. You have the self-improvement niche, you have the health and fitness niche, you have hobby related niches, and sports related niches. And if you go to Barnes & Noble or your local bookstore and you see that there's a magazine that targets that specific hobby. Are there magazines out there on how to build saltwater aquariums? If there's at least one magazine out there related to what you're passionate about, then that is a market you should go into.

What Markets Should You NOT Go Into?

And on the flipside of that, another common thing is when people say, "Oh, well, no one else is doing this, so now I can be the only one who does it and make a lot of money." And that's really not going to be true. If you don't see anybody else doing what you're passionate about, it's probably because it's not a profitable market, and you know, that can seem counterintuitive at first, but when I pick a market to go into, I want to go into a market that's competitive and has already proven that it's profitable, and not try to reinvent the wheel, or try something that no one else is doing.

And if you go into a market with no competition, there's probably no competition because there's no money being made. Sometimes you can find something out of the ordinary, of course, but generally if there's nobody already doing it, then it's probably not something you want to tackle at least for your first project. You want something that people are interested in, where people are spending money.

So make that list, check it out, look down the list, see what really turns you on, what you can talk about intelligently, or think about what you want to learn more about. Do some research and teach other people what you learn along the way.

The "Me" Niche

If you're stumped and just can't come up with a good niche, then work on the "me" niche. Start a blog and just start talking about your life. What did you do that day? What's your business? How about kids? Got any? Talk about parenting or what your kids are into. Have pets? Post pictures of them and tell stories about them.

There are so very many ways to make this work for you! And it will be fun!
Keeping your enthusiasm for working on your business every single day is the important part. You need to have something to work at that is interesting for you. With a "me" blog, you can connect with people who have similar interests and start bonding with an audience. All will begin to take shape as you continue writing in your blog every single day.

So what's the next step? After you pick a niche, you decide you want to be in the horse equipment niche, or whatever it is, you need to start thinking about setting up your business. So what would be the first step?

Chapter One Review

- ✓ Make a list of the things you already know or want to know more about
- ✓ Which topics are the most important to you? What are you passionate about?
- ✓ Don't automatically go into the "make money online" niche without realizing that the competition is stiff
- ✓ Go to a bookstore and check out the magazine section. If you see a magazine connected to the niche you want to pursue, it's probably a good bet.
- ✓ Do some research using Google's External Keyword Tool and see if people are searching for keywords related to your niche. Make sure that there are at least 10,000 actively searching for those keywords.
- ✓ If no niches jump out at you, set up a blog all about your life, the "me" niche.

Chapter Two:

Buying Your First Domain Name

After you decide on what niche you want to set your blog up under, the first thing you want to do is to get a domain name for your website, the place where people are actually going to go to and find your online presence.

A domain is also a Web address. You've undoubtedly seen them shown as http://www.sitename.com, http://sitename.com or www.sitename.com or not .com, but another extension such as .gov, .edu, .info, etc. These are called domain name "extensions," and which you choose is important. We'll talk about that in a moment.

But your domain will be YOUR place on the World Wide Web. -- a place that you can say easily and tell people where to find you. This goes back to just figuring out who you want to be. You need to figure out some keywords for your niche and you should use one of those in your domain name, even if it's general.

For example, if you want to be in the "dog training" niche, a domain with something about dogs in it is a good idea. "dogtraining.com" would be ideal, of course, but with so many people online these days, it's pretty hard to find a domain that specific. You may have to do some searching to find the domain you want.

FINDING YOUR PERFECT DOMAIN

It's really easy to search for domain names at places like Go Daddy (http://godaddy.com), Name Cheap (http://namecheap.com), or other sites that just help you to come up with something cool and applicable.

Tip: Don't pay more than $10 – 15 a year for your domain

One of these is Dot-o-Mater.com (http://www.dotomator.com/) where you can select different nouns and adjectives from a list they give you or you can plug in your own suggestions and come away with a very cool domain name. This site does some of the hard work for you.

Another site that will help you is "Bust a Name (http://www.bustaname.com/) where you can put in your own nouns and adjectives and it will come back with suggestions for you and tell you if the domain is available at various registrars and how much you will pay to register it.

The last option for finding your perfect domain name is Stuck Domains (http://www.stuckdomains.com/) where you can search and find expired domains or domains that are currently for sale. Sometimes, these domains will be a little more expensive, especially if they're really spot on about a niche. But some will work well for you while not breaking your bank.

We prefer to use GoDaddy.com for buying domains, as they're about as inexpensive as you can get. They're also one of the largest registrars and have a very solid reputation. Currently, a dot com domain name runs about $10 a year, though the price is creeping up – not due to the registrar raising prices, but ICANN (Internet Corporation for Assigned Names and Numbers) raising theirs.

ICANN is the policing system for domain names. Here's how the institution is described on their website at http://www.icann.org/ :

> "ICANN was formed in 1998. It is a not-for-profit public-benefit corporation with participants from all over the world dedicated to keeping the Internet secure, stable and interoperable. It promotes competition and develops policy on the Internet's unique identifiers.
>
> "ICANN doesn't control content on the Internet. It cannot stop spam and it doesn't deal with access to the Internet. But through its coordination role of the Internet's naming system, it does have an important impact on the expansion and evolution of the Internet."

And for this service, every domain has an additional charge. It's been going up of late, and will probably continue to rise over time. That's why we have mentioned the cost of a domain is $X "at this time."

Others use another site to register their domains, called "Name Cheap" (http://namecheap.com) or you can often use the hosting company where your domain will live, as many of them are registrars as well.

Important Factors to Consider

Reliability is very important when choosing a registrar, and GoDaddy is a very reliable company. You don't want to use a registrar that maybe isn't going to be around next week, or that's too expensive.

Back when the Internet was relatively new, domains cost more like $75 for the year, and some registrars are still selling domains at that high price. You really shouldn't pay more than $10 - $15 for an entire year.

The barriers to entry for actually having a physical online presence are so inexpensive compared to traditional business that it's ridiculous. In fact, you can get into online business for under $100.00 a month. And your business expense is something you must consider.

Many people online that think that you can make money on the Internet and not put out a dime. And you know, wish that were true, but there are certain elements that you've got to have and a domain name is definitely one of them.

So think about picking good domain name, something that's niche related, and then check the availability of the names you've brainstormed at any of the sites mentioned above.

Your Domain Extension Is Important

One thing to remember when choosing a domain is that it should be a dot com is you're going into business. Those are getting harder and harder to find, but the thing is, people still think "dot com." Anytime you give them a website they automatically think of that domain extension.

Other extensions that are okay, but not as good are "dot net," "dot org," "dot info," or your country extension, such as ".us." But dot com is definitely the most preferred, and I'd say "dot net" and "dot org" are okay. But try to stay away from anything else.

When you hear that a business has a website, like Pepsi or Starbucks, what do you naturally type into the address bar? www.Pepsi.com or www.Starbucks.com , right? That's exactly why having a .com domain is so important.

And one thing to point out again, is that it's going to be challenging. So the first time you sit down, I guarantee you that the first domain name you pick is not going to be available, nor is the second, or third, or fourth, or fifth, or sixth, or seventh, or eighth, or ninth, or tenth one. And probably it's going to take you about 20-50-100 different ideas of your own input before you find one that's available.

But don't worry, that's probably one of the hardest parts of establishing your online business, but just try to brainstorm some domain names that are going to be descriptive of what your niche is about, what your site is about. Make sure your domain name is easy to spell and it's easy to remember, and try to avoid using numbers for letters. Don't use the number 4 for the word for, or the number 2 for to because people might confuse that.

Be Sure Your Domain Describes You or Your Business

An example of a really good domain name is freecreditreport.com, which I'm sure looks familiar. You've seen those silly commercials on TV. Now, why is that such a good domain name? Well, it's a relatively short domain name, it's very easy to spell, it's very easy to remember, and it describes exactly what the website is about.

We know that this website called freecreditreport.com, it's not about how to lose weight, it's not about how to train your horse, or it's not about how to make sure your dog doesn't pee on the carpet, right? It's about credit reports and repairing your credit. So keep that in mind when you're creating or trying to find your domain name.

If you have a number in your domain name, you should try to see if the other spellings are available, like F-O-R, or F-O-U-R, you know, some people just really can't spell, and you might want to consider buying those domains as well so no matter what somebody types in, they will get to your website.

If You're in the "Me" Niche

If you're in the "me" niche, you want to get your name as a domain. If you have a name that lots of other people have, like John Smith or Jane Black, you could have a problem coming up with a .com name, as well.

Try some variations:

- Add your middle name
- Create "theRealYourName.com"
- Use your nickname or your full name
- Use your initials
- Use "YourName'sBlog.com"

There are lots of ways to get around that, and if you check with the domain tools that we mentioned earlier in this report, you should have no trouble coming up with a great domain name!

So that's a little bit about picking domains, but once you have a domain, then you have to decide where you're going to put it…

Chapter Two Review

- ✓ Do some brainstorming about your passions. What are they?
- ✓ Use one or a combination of the tools mentioned above to come up with a domain name that relates to your niche.
- ✓ Choose a reliable registrar that doesn't cost more than about $10 a year
- ✓ Try to come up with a .com domain
- ✓ If you're in the "me" niche, think about all the different ways you can use your own name as the domain.
- ✓ If your name isn't available in the way that you think of yourself, then brainstorm some other ways to get your name across. Use your middle initial, your full name with middle name, or just "The Real." Go Daddy is good at suggesting alternatives.

CHAPTER THREE:

CHOOSING A RELIABLE WEB HOST

Your domain name is the address of your business. So obviously, someone types in www.yourdomainname, that's how they get to your business, and your hosting is kind of how they get *inside* your business.

So when you upload your web pages, if you upload audios, if you upload videos, these are going to go into your hosting account, and sometimes you can get a hosting account with your domain name, or you can do it separately, and we're going to recommend that you get a separate hosting account because there's pluses and minuses of having a company that specializes in web hosting versus one that doesn't.

One of the main things you want to look for in a good web host is *reliability* because nobody can buy anything from you if your website is down. So a company that we recommend is Host Gator (http://hostgator.com), their reliability is stellar. Every web host goes down now and again, but they guarantee 99.9% uptime and that's been proven to be true, at least over the past few years that we've been recommending their service.

They know what they're doing. They're strictly a hosting company. Their support's great because you can call them up any time of the day or night, and they'll help you with your issues.

Shared vs. Dedicated Hosting

To start, you'll probably only need "shared" hosting. This means that your website and the websites of others will be on the same server. Dedicated hosting is more expensive, and until your company is much larger, it's really not that important. However, when you reach that level – when the traffic to your website is significant enough to require a more heavy duty plan, it's easy for Host Gator to move the files to a new server for you.

There are advantages to both types of hosting, but with shared hosting the cheaper price also includes more bandwidth, which is how much of your website information is transferred to visitors each month. Host Gator suggests that you think of bandwidth as gasoline for your car. When your bandwidth runs out, nobody can visit your site. Having unlimited bandwidth so that you never have to worry about it running out is a very good thing.

Host Gator also provides unlimited disk space. The more disk space you have, the more room for your files. With the advent of video storage, this became much more important. When you run out of space on the disk, you'll no longer be able to upload new files.

Host Gator also provides unlimited MySQL databases. These are important for some software programs that you may want to have on your site, such as blogs, forums, or membership sites. All of these require MySQL databases, and if your hosting plan doesn't include any, you won't be able to run any of the software that requires them.

So, the option is clear. You need enough bandwidth, disk space, and MySQL databases to get started. There are different levels of hosting at Host Gator, and as your business grows, you'll be able to upgrade whenever you wish.

> *One free and easy answer for an FTP program is to get the Mozilla Firefox Add-on called Firefox, and transfer files right from your Firefox browser.*

FTP (File Transfer Protocol)

When you begin uploading files to your web host, you can do it through their online file manager, which allows you to move files from your desktop computer onto their server. The only problem with this is that it's terribly slow; however, it's a bit more intuitive than using FTP (file transfer protocol) software to do the job. So, just to save time, it's a good idea to start off learning FTP right away.

One free FTP client that you can get is an add-on for a Firefox browser. Firefox is a very good, free browser option, and it will do a lot more for you, if you're planning to be a serious marketer. Though Internet Explorer is still used by many, there are several other options, including Chrome, Opera, Safari, and other browsers that work with either Windows or Apple computers.

Firefox will accommodate both operating systems, though there are separate versions for each. If you use this browser, one choice for a free FTP program is "FireFTP" and it opens right inside the browser. Here's how it looks:

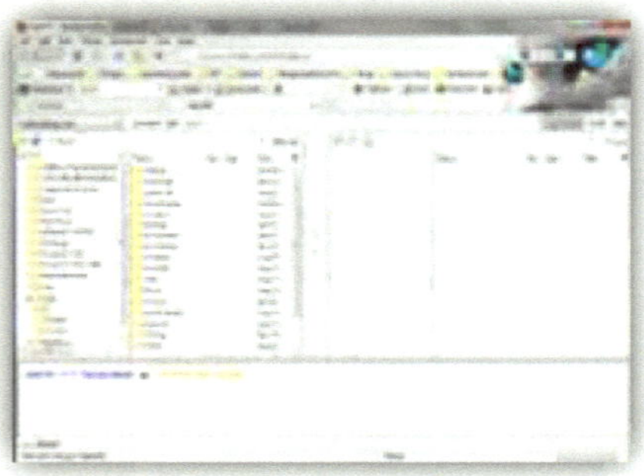

The files on the left side of the screen are on the desktop, and you simply find the file you need and drag it into your server account on the right. It's very simple once you get the hang of it.

The folder for uploading files to is called "public_html" or “httpdocs” Which folder you use depends on your hosting account. Here are examples of what you might see:

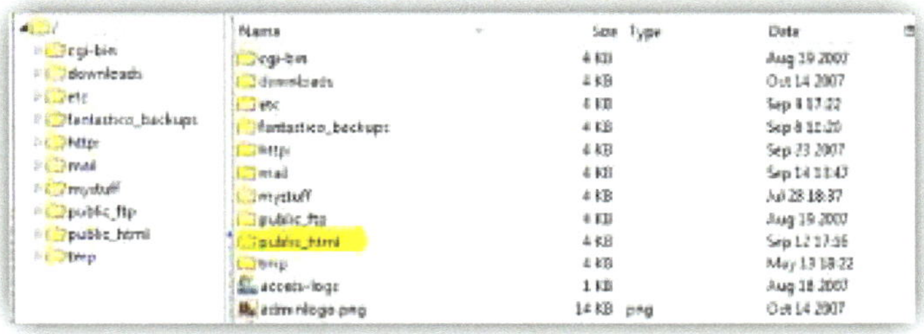

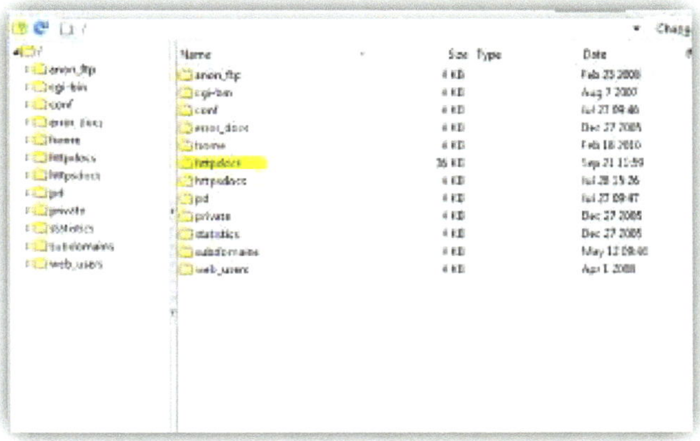

Some hosts use a folder called “www” but no matter what your hosting company calls the folder, it will be there and ready for you to use when you’re ready to upload your files. You don’t need to do anything for it to appear.

FTP Software

Other stand-alone free FTP software programs are Mozilla's Filezilla, Free FTP from the makers of Coffee Cup, and Easy FTP. After having used many different FTP programs, I can tell you that they all work the same way. There are paid software programs, as well, but they really don't work any better than the free ones.

But the best part about any of these programs is that will allow you to just transfer files from your desktop directly to your hosting account and it make it extremely fast, and really simple to get your stuff online.

Any hosting company has that ability, but I really like the way Host Gator lays everything out for you. You can see everything in their cPanel dashboard, which is your control panel more or less. You can add on domains from there, you can create email accounts so that your email comes from your domain, which we'll talk about later.

When I first started online, I tried all different hosting companies and the frustration of constantly having my websites down and unavailable was annoying. When that happens, if someone actually went to my website there was nothing there.

Trying to call customer support, or to get in contact with someone was a nightmare! Dealing with some type of one-man operation where the customer service hours were whenever they decided to be at home. It's like night and day dealing with a company like Host Gator where your website is up all the time, you can call their customer support 24 hours and speak with someone knowledgeable who can solve any problems that you have.

cPanel Hosting Benefits

cPanel has an element to it that's going to make installing your blog really easy and we'll talk about that too.

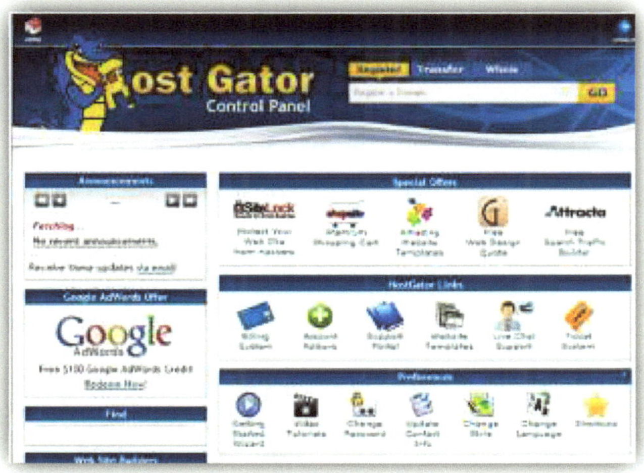

But people often wonder what kind of hosting to get because most companies offer Linux and they offer Windows, and PC people think, "Windows" because of Microsoft, right? A lot of people are going to Macs, but if you have a PC you might be thinking, "Oh, Microsoft, I have a PC. That's what I should do." That's not what you should do. You want Linux hosting and that's going to help you more with everything you do online. So Linux is the one you want to pick for sure, and like I said, with cPanel you're going to have PHP installers, which is what you're going to need to install your blog and they have programs to do that automatically.

So we're going to talk about that in just a minute, but another thing I touched on was you can create your own email accounts from your hosting account as well, and use your own domain.

Setting Your Nameservers or DNS

Unless you're hosting your domain at GoDaddy or another hosting company, you will need to "point" the domain that you just bought to the right servers. In other words, you'll need to tell GoDaddy where to send traffic when someone types in your domain name.

This is pretty simple to do. If you have Host Gator, you can find the appropriate servers in your cPanel dashboard or in the email that Host Gator sent to you when you opened the account. They look like this:

> NS629.HOSTGATOR.COM and
> NS630.HOSTGATOR.COM

The HOSTGATOR.COM portion of the DNS (dynamic name server) address will not change, only the server number, and each account has a specific address. Be sure to use the correct nameserver addresses or the transfer won't work.

To change the DNS from GoDaddy to Host Gator, go to "Domain Manager" at Go Daddy in the right-hand navigation panel.

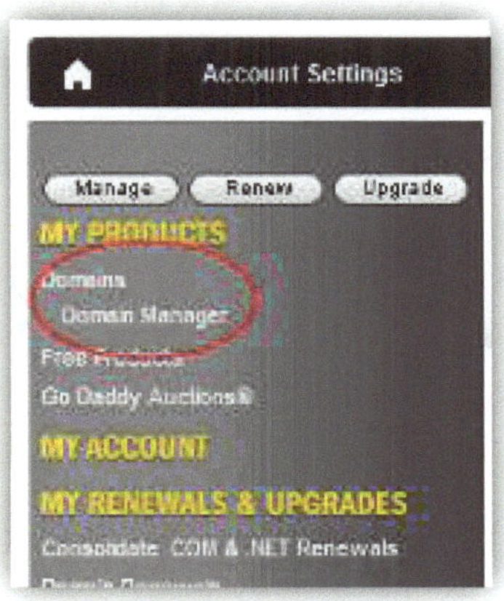

Find the domain you want to change servers for (at this point there is probably only one), and check the box next to it.

An icon that says "Nameservers" will brighten.

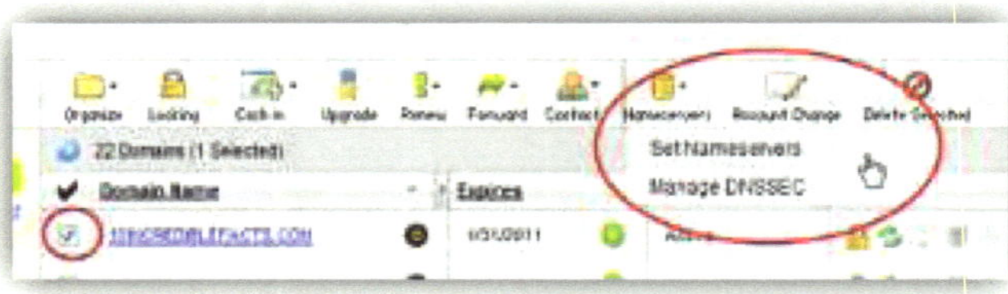

Click there, and you'll see a drop-down menu. Select "Set Nameservers."

A pop-up window will appear that looks like this:

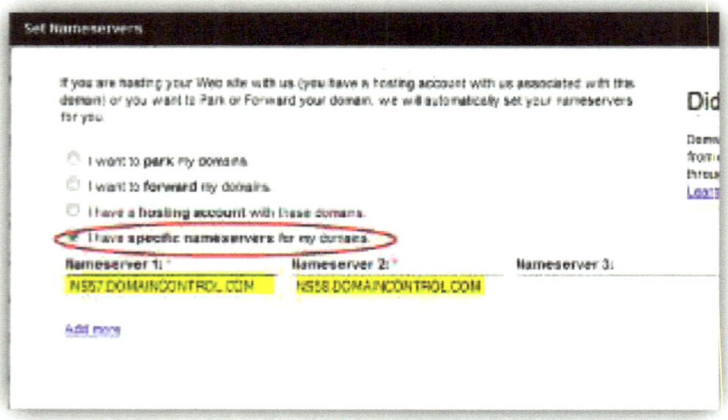

Select the radio button that says, "I have specific nameservers for my domain." You will see addresses already entered in the boxes. Simply replace them with your Host Gator nameserver addresses.

Because the Internet is so huge and growing every day, it will take a few minutes for the new addresses to "propagate," or take effect, so you will see a Go Daddy holding page until your domain "resolves." Usually this is well within 24 hours, but that's the time frame that GoDaddy and Host Gator give you for this to happen. If you live in a city, the time it takes can be under an hour. If you live in a remote area, it may be the whole day. Everyone's time frames will vary.

Once the change has taken effect, you will be able to type in your domain and go to your Host Gator account. Until you install your blog, you'll see a Host Gator holding page, so even if you don't have your site set up yet, you'll know that the DNS change has worked properly.

If for any reason this doesn't happen within the 24 hour period, check to see that you haven't mis-typed anything, and if you have an your domain still hasn't propagated, contact Go Daddy support. (The possibility that you'll need to do this is slim, if you have typed everything properly. Copy your nameserver addresses *exactly*.)

Create Email Accounts for Your Domain

If your domain is mydomain.com, you could have your first name at yourdomain.com, right? So that makes it really personal to you, personal to your business. You can create support emails or follow-up autoresponder messages that will have your personal email address on them when they're delivered, instead of Gmail or Yahoo, for example. It just makes your business look more legitimate.

You can create whatever email addresses you want to create just by going through your hosting account in cPanel and it's really, really simple to do. You click on a button, you tell them what you want the name of your email account to be, generate a password, and press create and it's there.

On your dashboard, click "Email Accounts:

The window on the next page will appear. Just fill in the name you want in front of your email address, a password, and your account is created. It really is that simple.

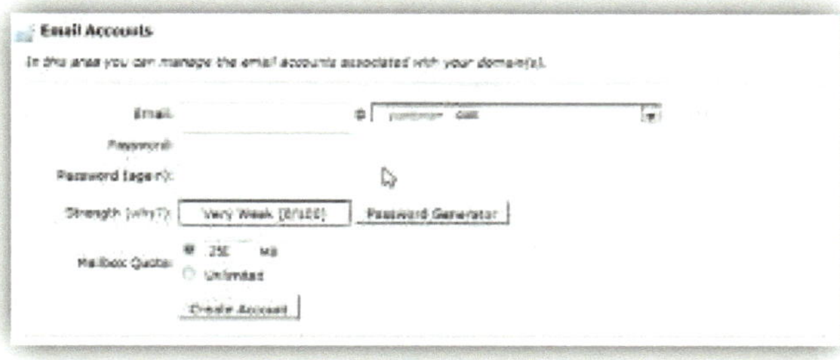

There are different platforms in different hosting companies. Another one is called Plesk. Rackspace, for example, uses Plesk and it's totally different from cPanel. It's setup differently, but it works pretty much the same way. It also has the ability to create databases and do all the things email accounts and all the things that you want to do, but that's another platform for hosting and it's not nearly as intuitive as cPanel. Here's what Plesk looks like:

So those are some things to think about when choosing a hosting company, and the biggest thing I think is finding a hosting company that's reliable -- not a one-man operation. You want a company that's been in the business a long time, a company that knows hosting, and a company that will keep your website running for you day after day after day.

Chapter Three Review:

- ✓ Be sure that your web host is reliable
- ✓ Acquire hosting that has cPanel access if you want to install your blog easily
- ✓ Once you select a host, set your nameservers (DNS or Domain name servers) to your specific hosting account addresses.
- ✓ Create email addresses for your domain, such as your personal address, a support address, etc. Be sure to note the usernames and passwords for your records and for configuring your email client
- ✓ You can read email messages from these accounts online or in your mail client, such as Outlook, but you will have to configure Outlook to work. Go to Tools/Accounts and fill in the appropriate information.

Chapter Four:

Installing Your WordPress Blog

WordPress blog software is one of the most popular blogging platforms out there, and one of the easiest to use. WordPress is what's known as "open source," which means that the source code is publicly accessible and that any developer can work on it and add refinements to the platform. It also indicates that the software is free.

This is really important because that means there's a huge community of people out there who are experts in WordPress and who are constantly working to make it better.

This also means that there are a lot of people creating different tools you can use with WordPress to make your websites better. Compare that model to using software that's put out by one company where it's a proprietary piece of software. In that case, you're basically held to the limitations of what that company wants to do with their software.

Using a tool like WordPress gives you ultimate freedom and flexibility in making a really good-looking website or blog. Plus, it allows you to do a lot of things that you want to do with it.

Plenty of Help Available

There's lots of free support for WordPress on their website, and because the software is so well-known and popular, there are tons of experts that you can tap into. If you're outsourcing, lots of people will help you do this stuff too, so you're not stuck with a limited platform that not a lot of people know how to use to limit your website's functionality, and also means that you'll probably have to pay extremely high prices for a custom programmer.

WordPress, very powerful platform, and at this point in time, I see no reason why anyone would choose to use anything but WordPress. It's also extremely customizable.

You can create just about any type website you want to using mostly free, but a combination of free and paid elements. If you want to pull in posts that are related to the post you're writing – there's a plugin. If you want to have Amazon affiliate products advertised – there's a plugin. If you want to send your posts directly to Twitter each time you write one – there's a plugin.

It's easy to see why WordPress is the best platform to use, bar none.

INSTALLING YOUR WORDPRESS BLOG

In the last chapter about hosting, we mentioned that you can install a WordPress blog within about five minutes, if you have a PHP installer included in your hosting package. Host Gator offers two types, one is Fantastico and the other is QuickInstaller, and both work pretty much the same way. There are other automatic software installation services, such as Elephante and all of them work almost the same way.

If you're a Host Gator customer or other cPanel hosting company customer, the first thing to do is to open your control panel, which resides at http://yourdomain.com/cpanel. You'll need to enter the username and password that you created when opening your hosting account, so be sure to have that in front of you before starting.

Once inside your dashboard, you'll see several icons in various sections. You're looking for the "Software/Services" portion of the page. QuickInstaller is listed first. The icon is a stopwatch with a swooping blue arrow, and the blue smiley face will be Fantastico. You only need to use one service, but Fantastico is the preferred service, and it will notify you of and install updates for you.

Fantastico's a nice little tool that makes doing very complex things, like programming a WordPress blog, very easy. So in the old days if you wanted to make a WordPress blog, you would have to go in there and know a lot of programming and installing a lot technical mumbo-jumbo, which if I actually talked about right now, it would probably fry your brain. But to make it simple, with Fantastico you can just click, add some basic information and install your WordPress blog. Fantastico really is a great tool.

Using Fantastico to Install Your Blog

So, let's talk about using Fantastico to install your WordPress software. Click on the blue smiley face to enter the Fantastico interface, and you'll come to a page with several different software installation options. If you have a "baby gator" account, you'll be able to install any of those programs, including shopping carts, forums, classified ads, CMS (content management systems), and so much more.

Today, let's concentrate on getting your WordPress blog operational. It's simple!

Click on WordPress in the "Blog" category, then "New Installation." If you have only one domain you won't have a choice, but if for any reason, you have more than one, a drop-down menu will appear and you can select the appropriate domain for your blog.

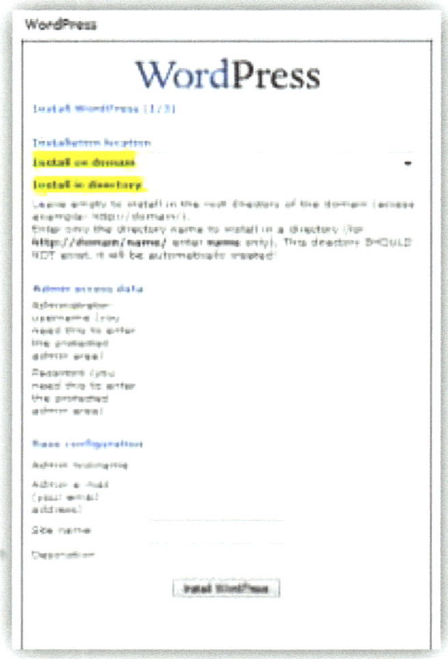

The next consideration is whether you want to install your blog on the root domain or in a sub-directory. So, for example, if you want the blog to be on http://yourdomain.com, you're all set. If you want to install it in http://yourdomain.com/blog, you'll need to complete the empty box that reads "Install in directory." If you want the URL to be as shown, type in "blog." If you want it to be another term like "recommends," then type that in and your blog's URL will be http://yourdomain.com/recommends.

Tip: Having your blog on a root domain means that people can type http://YourDomain.com and be at your blog. It's much easier for visitors to remember.

Having it on the root domain makes it really easy for people to get to your blog. They just type in your domain and BOOM! They're right at your blog. If you really don't want to have more than one domain (which that's probably not going to last long, as your business grows or as you become more involved with Internet marketing, you're probably going to own several domains. But in the beginning, you know, it's just really up to you which way you do it.

And if you want to have, say a squeeze page, which we'll also talk about later on as the front door of your blog, then you're going to want the blog in a subdirectory. But you need to decide that before you install it, or you're going to have problems down the road.

My advice is just to install the blog on your root domain.

The next step is to **type in your administrator username**. It can be anything you choose: admin, your first name, a code word, etc. Then, type in a password and be sure to write both down. A password with both lower- and upper-case letters and digits will be the most secure.

Next, **enter an email address** for your blog. This can be an address that you've created for your domain. (See Chapter 3: Create Email Accounts for Your Domain.) It should be a valid address so that you can have the installation information emailed to you. Print that out and save it with your other important information.

You will also need to **name your blog and provide a description**. You can use something simple here for now, as we will discuss proper naming and how it affects your place in the search engine results pages in a later chapter. For now, it really doesn't matter, so just choose something easy and move along to the installation.

After you have completed all of the information, click on "Install WordPress" and Fantastico will install your blog in a matter of just a few minutes.

You are now the proud owner of your first WordPress blog… Congratulations!

Installing WordPress from Scratch

In case you already have a hosting company and Fantastico isn't available, you can always install a blog from scratch, and it's really not that difficult.

The first thing you need to do is to create a MySQL database in your hosting account. If you don't have MySQL database availability, you will definitely need a better or different type of hosting account on a Linux server.

If you do have that availability, just create a new database. Some hosting accounts, like Host Gator for example, have a MySQL wizard that walks you through the steps. You name your database, give it a username and password and you're all set. Be sure to keep this information because you will need it later on for the WordPress installation. Keep it close!

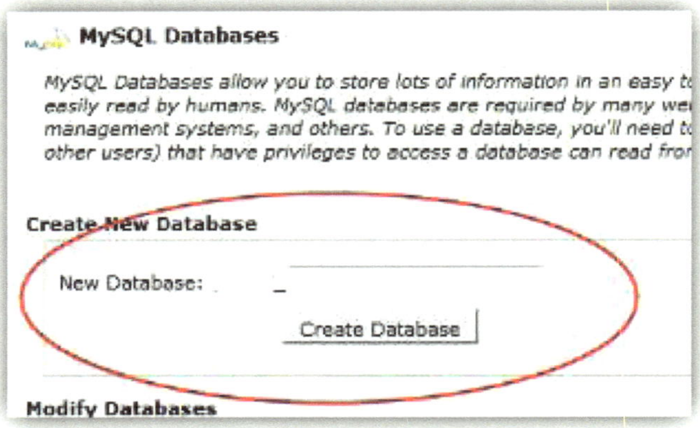

The next step is to download the software. Don't confuse WordPress.com with WordPress.org. The former is a hosted blogging solution where you can set up a free blog, but you really don't want that. The biggest reason is that WordPress doesn't want commercially-oriented blogs on their service. If you put so much as an affiliate link on your blog, when WordPress finds out, your blog will be shut down and you'll have to recourse or access to any of the information on it.

Neither can you have an opt-in form on a WordPress.com blog, so that defeats your whole marketing system. Stay with a blog on your own hosting account and your chances of success go up exponentially.

Hosted blogging solutions are great for people just wanting to communicate with the world about their lives, their pets, or other interests. However, they are completely unacceptable for business because they don't permit commercialism and if you try to include affiliate links in your posts or to sell anything from your blog, the host can simply shut you down without recourse. All of your information will be lost. If you're serious about making money online, a WordPress on your own hosting account is very important to have.

Once you have the software downloaded, unzip the files using a program like WinZip or another extractor. It's time to upload WordPress!

Log into your site via FTP, and decide where you want the blog to reside. If it's in the root domain, you can open the outside folder for WordPress and you'll see three folders: wp-admin, wp-content, and wp-includes and a bunch of other files. Select all of them and drag them into your root domain.

If you're installing the blog in a subdirectory, create a new folder and upload the WordPress folders and files into that folder.

Inside the WordPress folder, you'll also see a file that says "config_sample.php." You need to edit that file, so get an HTML editor opened or a simple text editor for that activity.

You will need the information for the database you created in your hosting account now.
This is the ONLY section you need to worry about.

```
// ** MySQL settings - You can get this info from your web hos
/** The name of the database for WordPress */
define('DB_NAME', 'database_name_here');

/** MySQL database username */
define('DB_USER', 'username_here');

/** MySQL database password */
define('DB_PASSWORD', 'password_here');

/** MySQL hostname */
define('DB_HOST', 'localhost');

/** Database Charset to use in creating database tables. */
define('DB_CHARSET', 'utf8');

/** The Database Collate type. Don't change this if in doubt.
define('DB_COLLATE', '');
```

Fill in the name of your database where you see, 'database_name_here,' your username where you see, 'username_here,' and your password where you see 'password_here.' OVERWRITE these, so that 'database_name_here' becomes 'theActualNameofYourDatabase'. However, change NOTHING else. If you do, your blog won't work.

Rename the file you just edited to “config.php.” and upload it to your root domain or to the folder where you uploaded the wordpress folders and files.

Now, go to the address of your blog: http://yourdomain.com/wp-admin/install.php or http://yourdomain.com/blog/wp-admin/install.php, and follow these steps:

a. Enter the blog title
b. Enter your email address
c. Click install
d. Save the password or you may not be able to find it again. Have it emailed to you, as well.
e. Click on login

Use the username and password that you just created to log into your dashboard.

You can always log into your blog by clicking in the sidebar widget that says, META. (Usually the last widget at the bottom.) or go to http://yourdomain.com/wp-admin or if the blog is in a subdirectory, go to http://yourdomain.com/subdirectory/wp-admin and you’re in!

In the next chapter, we’ll explore the WordPress dashboard and make sure you’re familiar with how your WordPress blog works.

CHAPTER FOUR REVIEW

- ✓ Get acquainted with cPanel at Host Gator or your personal hosting account.
- ✓ Find the section that contains Software/Services and *Fantastico*
- ✓ Complete the necessary information and install your WordPress blog
- ✓ If you do not have cPanel hosting, follow the steps above to create a database and install WordPress from scratch.
- ✓ Create a database in cPanel and put your username and password aside
- ✓ Download the current version of WordPress
- ✓ Upload it to your server
- ✓ Change config_sample.php to config.php and add the appropriate details for your server

CHAPTER FIVE:

YOUR WORDPRESS BLOG

First, let's explain that all WordPress dashboards look the same right out of the box. However, you can customize what you see very easily and when you're done, it may not look like anyone else's at all.

Also let it be said that WordPress changes rather rapidly. At the time of this writing we're working with WordPress 3.0.1, which means they made one revision to the current version. But that can change.

I'm going to show you how things work with what we have now, and the labels and most of the information will never be different. Just know that what we'll go over in this chapter is in regard to aspects that are important to know and will probably always be the same.

To log into your blog, all WordPress blogs have the same log-in page, and the URL looks like this: http://yourdomain.com/wp-admin. Type in the username and password that you used when you installed the blog, and then you're inside.

YOUR DASHBOARD

WordPress is laid out pretty simply, and it's very easy to get around. But some people are a little nervous about it. They look at it the first time and think, "Oh, my goodness. What's all that?" But it's really not that difficult.

The most important parts are where to post, how to add pages, how to change your theme and how to add plugins to customize your blog. The good news is that it's all point and click, there are no technical skills involved.

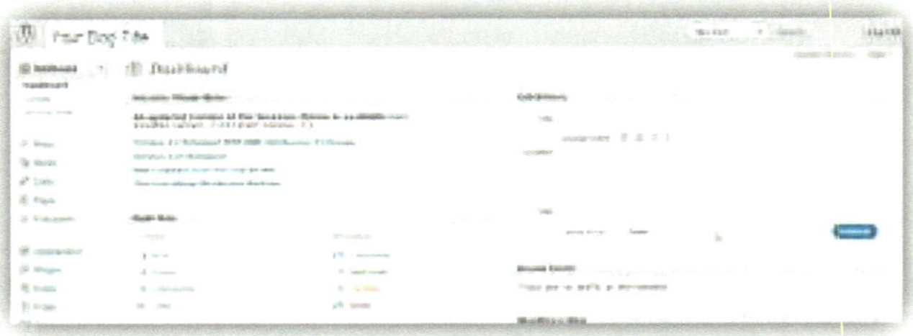

In fact, it's just like a riding a bike. The first time you get in there, you're going to be unfamiliar with what's there. You might be a little nervous and think, "Am I going to break something if I do something wrong?" But once you play around with it more and get more familiar with it, you're going to find it's really easy, user-friendly interface and the thing I encourage people to do is just get inside and start clicking the buttons and see what they do, and don't be afraid to break it. You can't!

Start playing around with the interface, and what you'll find is that even if there are lots of different options, and many different things you can do, over time you're probably going to land on a set of core things that you do on a very regular basis -- that you do over and over again. And we're going to talk about some of those activities, like, making posts, updating your blog, and things like that shortly. For now, let's go over your dashboard.

The Left-Side Navigation Panel

This is where all the meat for your blog lives. First you have a section for the dashboard itself. Here's where Akismet (a spam protector plugin that we'll talk about in a later chapter) stats live. You can check them to see how many posts the spam blocker has handled for you, but it's not terribly important. You probably won't spend much time checking that out.

This section is also where your "Updates" will appear. When a new update comes along for WordPress, a plugin, or a theme, you'll see a black circle with a white number inside showing how many updates there are available. Take care of these right away!

Usually, plugins update most frequently, but WordPress updates are critical. Be sure to backup your database before upgrading to a new version of WordPress so that you don't lose anything, first. We'll talk more about that in a minute, but always keep that in mind.

New versions of WordPress may not work with one or more of your plugins or your theme, so it's always smart to keep your blog backed up. There is a plugin that will do it on a regular basis for you, so keep reading.

Posts

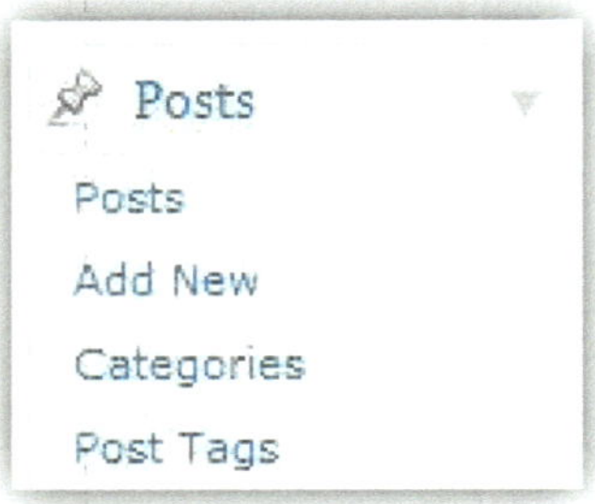

The "Posts" section is where you will add posts, edit posts, create categories for your posts, and where you can see your post tags. You can click on any of those links to perform the actions they lead to. In the tags category, you can also see a "tag cloud," which will show you what your most dominant tags are.

Media

The "Media" section is where all of your images and videos that you place in your blog will live, and you can find them in the "library," in case you want to use them more than once.

Links

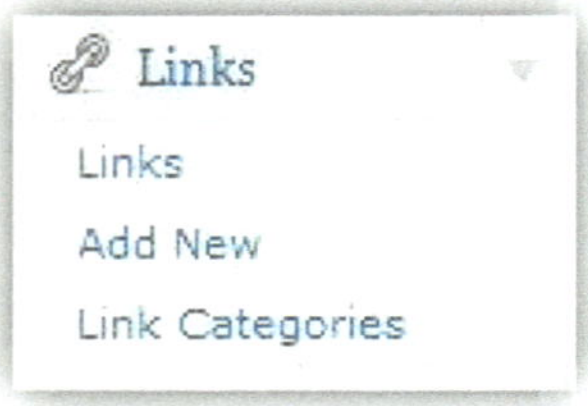

The "Links" section is where you can place links to other blogs, affiliate products, other websites that you own, or other websites that are closely related to your niche. You can also create categories for your links.

PAGES

The pages section allows you to see pages you have already created and add new pages. Pages are similar to posts, but are usually seldom updated. So, for example, an About page, Frequently Asked Questions page, or Privacy Policy can all be created as Pages, rather than posts.

COMMENTS

The Comments section is where you can see all the comments that people have made about your posts in the past. You'll also see new comments that need approval and spam comments that the Akismet plugin has captured for you. It's good to look at those to be sure that Akismet isn't' picking up valid comments, but the software is generally right on and as you train it, it gets better and better at keeping the spam out of your blog.

APPEARANCE

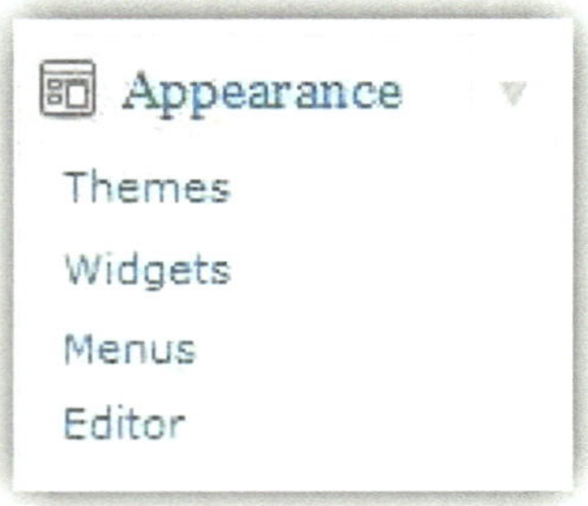

The "Appearance" section is important because it's where you will change themes, add widgets, and create menus. If you're familiar with PHP, it's also where you can edit your theme to accommodate your needs.

PLUGINS

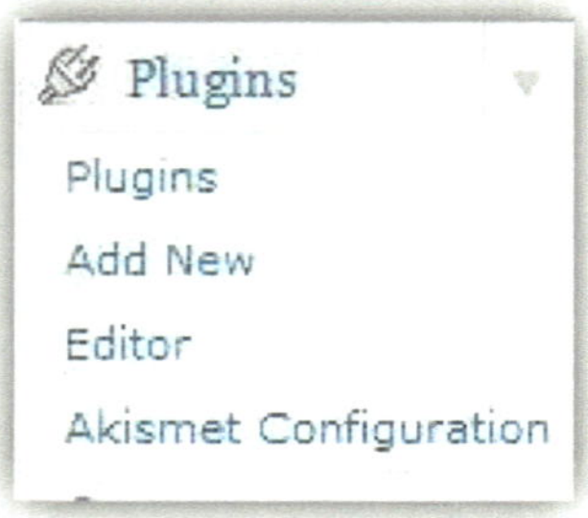

The "Plugins" section is where you can see the plugins that are installed and add new plugins. You can also edit the plugins from this section, if you're familiar with PHP. Otherwise, this is a section I'd leave alone. Changing one small thing in a plugin could cause it to stop working.

This is also where the Akismet Configuration is located. We'll talk more about plugins and activating them a future chapter.

Users

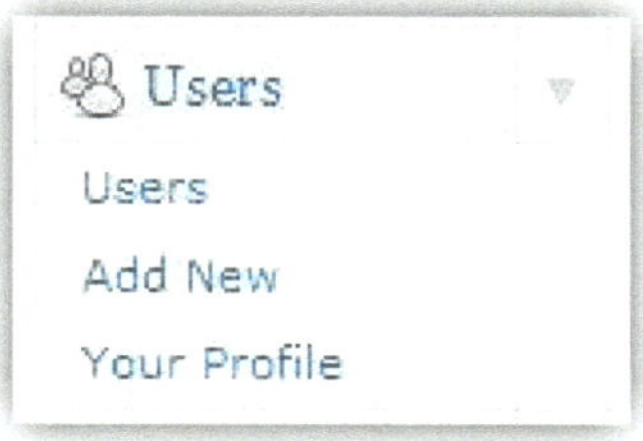

Here is where you can add users to your blog. You can allow subscribers, authors, and administrators all have a unique login to the blog. It's also where you create your own profile and change the color scheme of your blog from grey to blue.

Tools

WordPress provides a couple of tools that aren't that useful. One is a "Press This" button that allows you to post to your blog with a touch of the widget. You may find this useful.

The other tools allow you to convert tags to categories and vice-versa.

The most important aspects of this section are “Import” and “Export.” These will be useful when importing content from another blog or exporting your content for a backup.

SETTINGS

This section of your dashboard is very important, so let’s go over each element in detail:

✓ *GENERAL*

This is where you set your name for the blog and its tag line. These are akin to your title and description for a web page. You should use a primary keyword in your title and description first. The rest is up to you.

On this page, also set your time zone, and new users’ roles, which should be subscriber, unless you specifically want other people to be able to mess with your blog (not a good idea). Set your date and time format here, too.

✓ *WRITING*

The most important part of this page is the “Update Services” at the bottom of the page. WordPress will “ping” blog directories for you. Keep this in mind, as we’ll be giving you something important to add here in a future chapter.

- ✓ *READING*

  Here, you will decide whether you want a static front page for your blog or updating posts. The latter is more traditional, but either way works. You'll also decide whether you want to show the entire post or a summary for each.

- ✓ *DISCUSSION*

  There are several preferences in regard to blog commenting that you can fill in according to your own preferences. One aspect that should be considered is the part that reads: "Before a comment appears…." If you want to avoid spam or derogatory comments from hitting the front of your blog, be sure to check, "An administrator must always approve the comment," and uncheck "Comment author must have a previously approved comment." This way, you'll see every comment that is made and decide whether or not it will appear on your blog.

- ✓ *MEDIA*

  In the "Media" section, you can set thumbnail sizes for your images and other image-related information. This is personal preference, so don't spend too much time worrying over this. There is no right or wrong way to complete this. Just be sure that your images are large enough to see when added to a post, and not too large to bog it down.

Large images take up major bandwidth. If you scan a photo or use one from a digital camera, they can be quite large. Before adding these to your blog, pull them into a graphics editing software like Windows Paint or a similar program for the Mac. A free graphics design program that is much like Adobe Photoshop is called Gimp, which you can pick up here: http://www.gimp.org/. It's free. But if you're not used to working with that sophisticated a program, you can also use Google's Picassa at http://picasa.google.com/ (which comes in Windows and Mac versions) or any other photo editing software you like to change your image sizes. This is very important to keep your blog running smoothly.

✓ *Privacy*

Here's where you decide if you want your blog to be available to the public or to be private and invisible to search engine spiders. If you're building a site, you may want to use the private option, until your blog is ready. Or, if you're using a blog to store sensitive documents, this is another important page to consider.

✓ *Permalinks*

This is another important page. You need to set your permalinks to help your search engine optimization value. So, rather than allowing WordPress to dictate your permalink, which will look like this by default: http://yourdomain.com/?postnumber, it's better to have a keyword in your permalink. These lead to the single post pages in your blog.

Blog posts are constantly updating, if you're blogging religiously, as you should be. As new posts happen, old posts disappear to your archives. That's why single post pages are important and since search engine spiders view each post as a separate web page, you want to set each post up properly. We'll talk about a plugin that helps you do this in a future chapter, but for now, start by creating a search-friendly permalink structure.

Be sure that whatever permalink structure you choose that it picks up the post's title, which should include a keyword phrase its the beginning to assure search engine engagement.

It's important to do this when setting up your blog or search spiders will think that the old permalink pages are just missing. Not good.

What you want to do is tell your blog that each new permalink should have a post identifier and the title to your post.

Since all posts should have a keyword that's important to the post up front in the title, this makes your permalink more valuable in terms of search.

Click the last radio button, labeled "Custom Structure," and insert this code exactly:

/%post_id%/%postname%/

Save and you need never think about it again.

Summing It All Up

Your blog settings are important for many reasons as you've no doubt learned in this chapter. You have to tell WordPress how you want it to behave – how your blog should be titled, what type permalink to use, and whether you should approve comments. Most of these will be set once and then you never have to worry about them, so be sure to do it before starting to blog.

All of the right side sections in your blog will be important to you at one time or another, so click through and check them out. Get familiar with how things are set up and then, start thinking about more interesting things like how you want your blog to look and what topics you'll want to post. It's just that simple. If you want to collapse the right-side navigation panel, you can click any of the arrows that sit between each section. I have highlighted

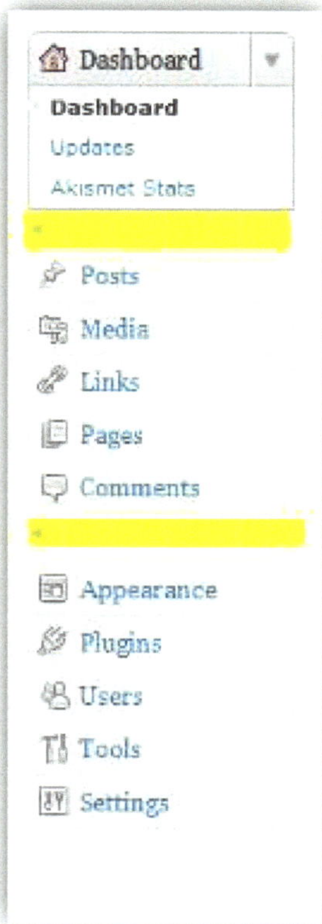

them here for you:

The only other part of the dashboard that might interest you is on the upper-right-hand side, and looks this way:

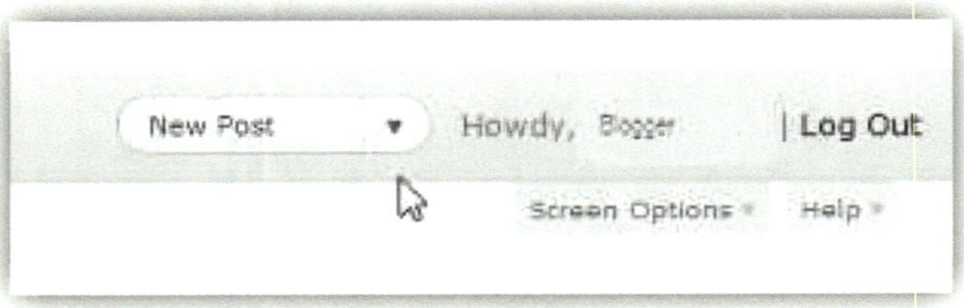

You can open "New Post" and get to drafts, comments and more. You can also set "Screen Options" and tell WordPress what you'd like to see when you log into your dashboard.

The other cool thing about WordPress is that all elements are draggable. So, for example, you can change the position of your "quick post" blank to be on the left instead of the right. Anytime you rest your cursor and see a four-way arrow, you can move what it's touching.

One very cool thing about WordPress is that it's so customizable. You can make it look just the way you want it to, and it's pretty simple!

In our next module, we'll talk about changing your blog's appearance. Having a theme that suits your business and isn't the same as what everyone else has is really important, so let's move on…

Chapter Five Review

- ✓ Log into your blog's administration area.
- ✓ Open each navigation panel and become acquainted with what's inside
- ✓ Create a great title and tag line for your blog. Be sure to use a main keyword first in both. If you're working in the "Me" niche, that should be your name.
- ✓ Be sure to check the box in the "Discussion" section that allows you to approve all comments coming into the blog.
- ✓ Don't forget to resize large images, such as those you get from a digital camera or scanner.
- ✓ Change your permalink structure so that it's more search friendly.

Chapter Six:

Personalizing Your Blog

One of the most appealing aspects of having a WordPress blog is that it's completely customizable. You can make it look any way you want to. Or, you can turn it into a sales page or a squeeze page or whatever. It's just amazing.

But the most amazing part about all of that is that WordPress makes it so easy for you to find different plugins to make your blog behave the way you want it to. It's also easy to install them, and you can create any type atmosphere that you want with your blog by changing the way it *looks*. So, let's start with themes so that you can get yourself going more quickly.

Changing your theme

The very first thing you want to do is change your blog theme. Using the one that came with the blog just screams, "Newbie!" and you don't want that. You want to be professional, if you want people to trust you and do business with you.

And the cool thing is that you can do that right from your blog!

You'll notice that on the left side of every page is a navigation panel that will take you to different functions within the blog. Go to the tab that says, "Appearance" and click:

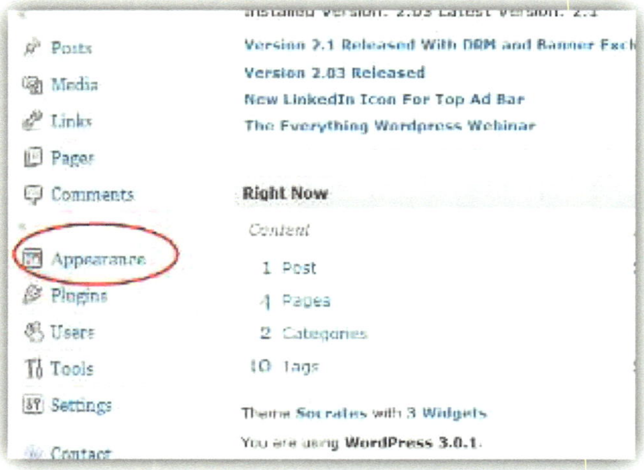
Posts
Media
Links
Pages
Comments
Appearance
Plugins
Users
Tools
Settings
Contact
Version 2.03 Released
New LinkedIn Icon For Top Ad Bar
The Everything Wordpress Webinar
Right Now
Content
1 Post
4 Pages
2 Categories
10 Tags
Theme Socrates with 3 Widgets
You are using WordPress 3.0.1.

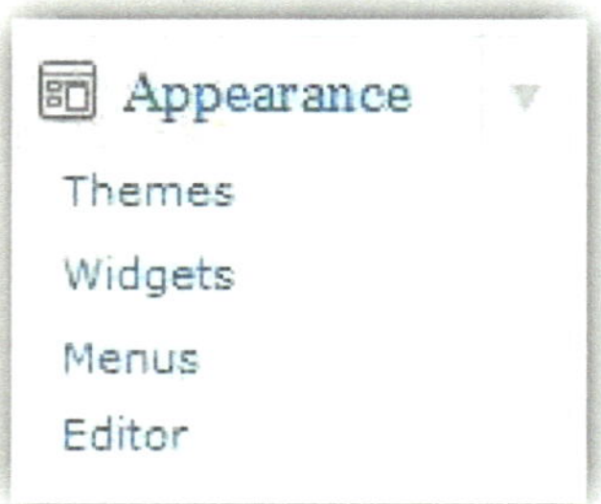
Appearance
Themes
Widgets
Menus
Editor

Next, click "Themes," and you'll arrive at the page below:

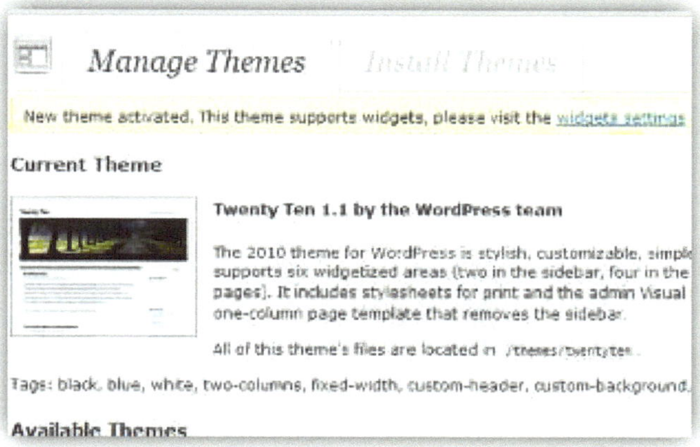

Click on the tab at the top that says, "Install Themes," and you'll arrive at a page that looks like this:

Get More Customers, Fans, Readers and Sales
in the Easiest Way Possible!
Watch The Video Now:
http://TheInternetSellingSystem.com

As you can see, you can choose from several different colors, the number of columns you want in your theme, the width and different features.

One important fact to keep in mind is that you want a right-hand sidebar. Search engine spiders search from left to right and down, so they will read your left-side column first, and figure nothing is new. They might just move on. You don't want that!

Unless you purchased a specialized theme, like DIY's *Thesis*, for example that is specially designed for great SEO, stick with a right-side column.

Here's an example of how a results page looks when you make a theme query:

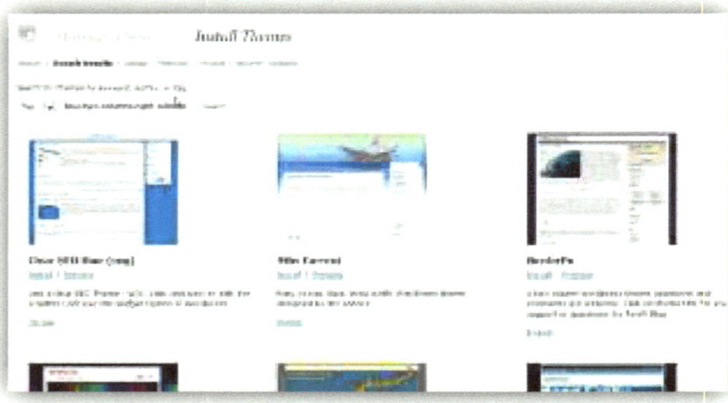

The themes that you can find through your blog will be free themes, and there are thousands to choose from. If you can't find what you're looking for, you can also go to http://WordPress.com/extend/themes and complete your search there.

If STILL nothing turns you on, you can search for the term "free WordPress themes" in Google and you'll find all the free themes you can imagine.

Yet, if you're interested in being unique, there are lots of sites that sell custom and very fancy themes that will suit any taste.

Some paid themes are not just interesting but will help the search engines to find your blog and to allow it to rank in the search engines. You can find themes like DIY's *Thesis*, Joel Comm's *Socrates*, themes from Studio Press or Woo Themes, and many, many others. These themes are priced between around $60 to hundreds of dollars, so if you're building your business on a shoestring, this is something you may want to decide on later.

Installing Your New Theme

Installation is simple if you choose a theme that you searched from your blog. You click on the theme you want, a lightbox window will pop-up, which will allow you to preview how the theme will look on your blog. If you like it, close the preview window and click "Install." It's that simple.

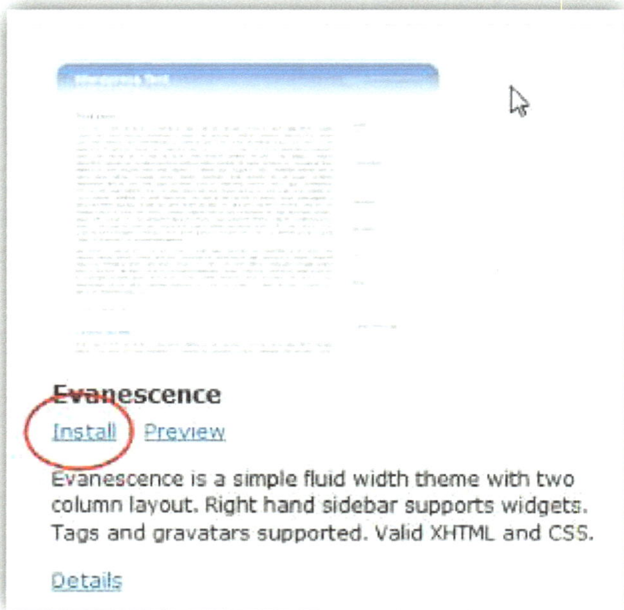

If you found a theme at WordPress.org or another site on the Web, it's still easy to install in the "Install Themes" tab, you'll see a link on the right-hand side that says, "Upload."

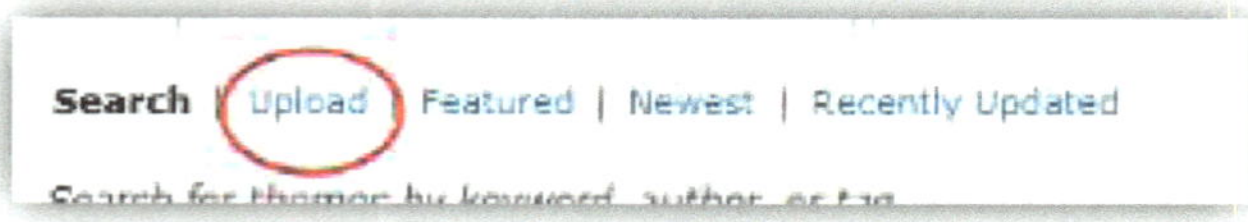

When you click there, a new tab opens that will allow you to navigate to the theme file, upload it and install it from there. Simple!

But if you want to be techy, you can do it the old way – via FTP. First, unzip the file, and go to the inner folder. Upload that folder

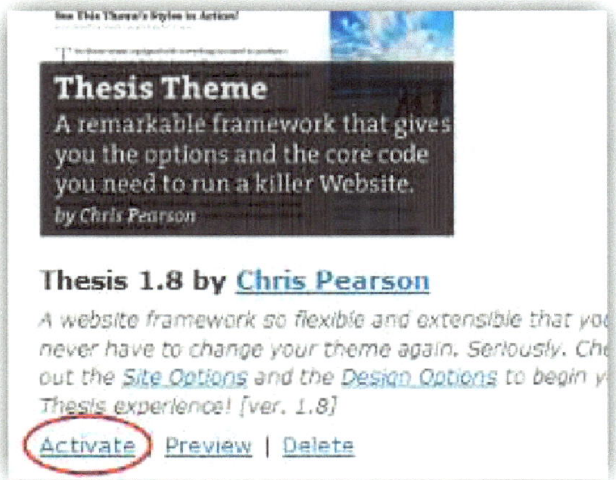

to wp-content/themes. Then, go to your blog, appearance and themes, and activate the new theme. Still easy!

Follow Your Niche

Regardless of what theme you choose, unless it's simple colors, be sure that it's congruous with your niche. For example, if you're in the "gardening" niche, don't use a theme with kittens on it. That won't make sense. Find a nice theme that has plants on it, perhaps.

Or, if you're in the football niche, don't have a "technical" looking theme. Find something related to football.

But if you're in the "Me" niche, any theme can apply. The best kind will have an image of your smiling face.

Whatever you choose, be sure that it's clean and neat and that you can enjoy while still appealing to the folks in your niche.

Otherwise, go for it and have fun!

Be creative, but not distracting. Remember, in business, plain usually works better than too fancy.

Chapter Six Review

- ✓ Log into your blog administration area.
- ✓ Go to the Appearance section in the left-side navigation panel.
- ✓ Choose Themes
- ✓ Select the "Install" tab at the top of the screen
- ✓ Choose from the many options for color, etc.
- ✓ Be sure to choose "right-side" columns
- ✓ Preview the themes you like.
- ✓ Go back to the install tab and click "Install" to activate the theme you have chosen.
- ✓ You can also search for WordPress themes at http://wordpress.org/extend/plugins
- ✓ To upload a zipped theme, choose "upload" from the Appearance/Themes/Install tab.
- ✓ Browse to where the theme is on your hard drive, and allow your blog to install it.

Chapter Seven:

Customizing Your Blog

One of the reasons that WordPress is such an amazing software is that it's open source, as we discussed early on. Anyone can work on the code to create innovative new tools to make WordPress exactly what you want it to be – not just to look like, but you can have it behave the way you want it to, as well. And even cooler than all that… most of the tools that make WordPress do what you want it to are free. Free!

Actually adding plug-ins to your blog is really kind of fun because there's so many plug-ins out there. So, think of it this way: If you've ever said to yourself, "I want to have this on my blog," or "I saw another blog that had this. How did they do that?" Chances are they did it with a plug-in.

So you can put plug-ins in your blog that get more visitors to your website. You can get plug-ins that will help you build your list faster. You can get plug-ins that will help you put advertisements on your website so you can make money. There are really plug-ins for just about everything, but there's a core group of plug-ins, and there's literally tens of thousands of plug-ins out there. I mean, we could go on about plugins for pages. But for the purposes of this book, there are a few key plug-ins that you should absolutely have installed in your blog as a core fundamental.

How to Find Plugins

So first of all, let's talk about how you actually find plug-ins and put them onto your website.

On your left-side navigation panel, inside your WordPress blog, look for the little button that says "Plug-ins." And then click on "Add New."

Once you get to the screen that says "Install Plugins," you can

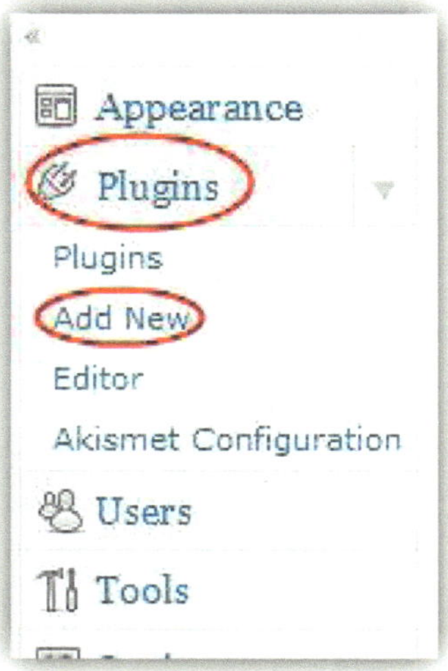

do a search for the name of the plug-in that you're looking for.

When you type in terms for the plugin you're looking for, you'll get a new page with several options. If I were looking for a plugin that added related posts to my blog, the results page would look like this:

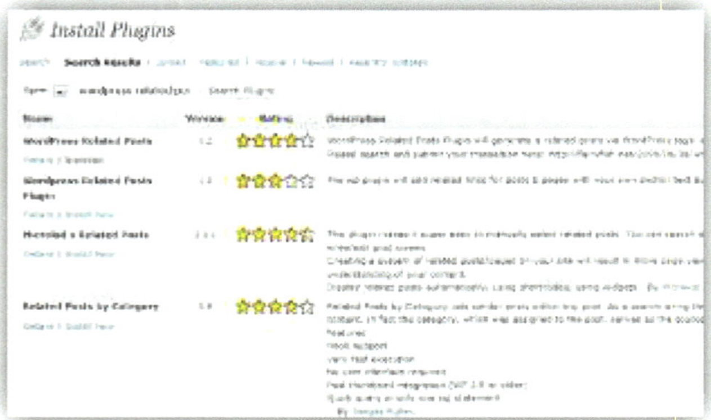

You'll notice that each plugin has a rating from users, and under its name, you'll see two links. The first is to get more details about the plugin, and the second is a link that says, "Install." All you have to do is click that link, and the plugin will install itself.

The *first time* you install a plugin or a theme, you'll need to give your blog your FTP information, so have your username and password close at hand. Once you have entered it, you will probably never need to do that again. It's that simple!

Configuring Your Plugins

With some plug-ins, there are some additional steps you need to do to set up that plug-in to work properly, and usually, it's very easy to do. One of them comes right along with WordPress.

Everyone knows what spam is in regard to email, but did you know that your blog can also be spammed? It's called comment spamming and there are lots of nefarious tools out there that gather blog addresses and send comments with absolutely NO meaning in order to get backlinks for the spammers' blogs.

WordPress has a plugin that comes right along with the blog software, called Akismet, that's a pretty good spam filter. It's a smart plugin that determines which comments are spammy and which ones should be reviewed. (Remember that we said in a previous chapter that you should be approving all comments that come into your blog, and this is the reason.)

Trust me, Akismet is one of the most valuable plugins there is because once you have a blog up, you're a target. People are going to try and post junk on there. They're going to post nonsense. They're going to try to send links to their Viagra websites and to their x-rated websites, and we see this all the time. Actually, the same nonsense you see in your inbox, is what people are going to try and put onto your website. Akismet will stop that from happening, and since it's a smart plugin, it will get better and better at it over time.

Your WordPress API Key

Akisment will require that you do some extra work to make it work on your blog. It's not hard, and if you know how to do it, it's really no big deal at all. You need what's called an "API" key, which used to be free. Very recently, Akismet when to a paid version for business owners, and using the plugin will cost $5 a month if you have one blog or more if you have several.

If you want to skip the expense, you can find plenty of other spam filter plugins at http://WordPress.org/extend/plugins that remain free. Choose those with 5-star ratings and install them as I showed you above.

However, since Akismet is a leader in spam detection, you may choose to continue with that plugin. So, the first thing to do is to activate that plugin.

From the left-side navigation panel, go to “Plugins,” and all of your installed plugins will show up on that page. Right now, you’ll probably see two, one is Akismet and the other is “Hello Dolly.” Hello Dolly is someone at WordPress’s idea of a prank, it seems. All it does is add a line from the song “Hello Dolly” to the top of your admin area every time you open the blog. If you love the song, that’s cool. If not, you can just delete that plugin.

You want the label “Akismet Configuration,” which is the page where you will enter your WordPress API key:

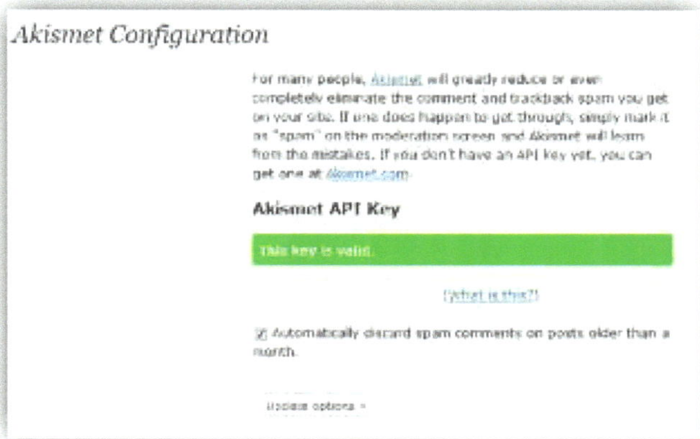

All-in-One SEO Pack

There is another plug-in, but it is critical for you to have. Good search engine optimization really is the Holy Grail of online free traffic, so having this plugin is very important and you need to use it every time you post in your blog, and All-in-One SEO allows you to add a title and description to every post you make, which is critically important to search engine spiders.

I don't want to get too technical about this, okay, and I don't want to explain why this is important or anything because you're just starting out. You will find out why in the months and years to come. But anything that you can do to help the search engines find your posts and, you know, read them and go through them, the better. And the more you use the keywords that you've chosen the better.

After you finish creating your post, you're going to go to this All-in-One plug-in, it shows up underneath the post area, and you just type in your title, description, and appropriate keywords.

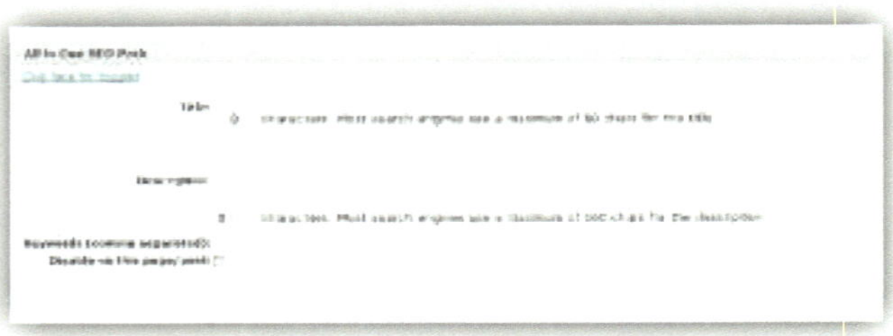

WordPress Database Backup

WordPress Database Backup is a plug-in that will back up all your blog posts, comments, images, etc. It will store them on your hosting account server, or it will email the back-up to you at a schedule that you determine. You don't have to do anything but set it and forget it, and it's very important to have.

Hackers sometimes choose random accounts to hack into and wreak havoc. Your entire blog could be compromised, and you could lose everything that you took so long to build. So, this plugin is NOT one you want to overlook.

You can use all of the default settings (default means the way the programmer intended), or you can modify those in your left-side navigation panel, under Tools/Backup.

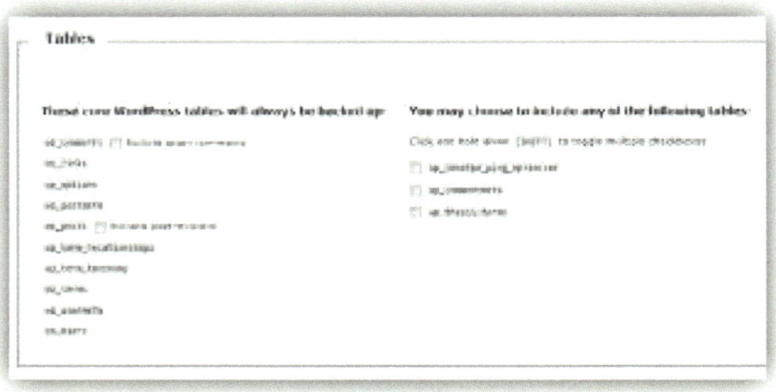

In this section, you can see on the left side that every important table in your database is already covered. If you want your comments backed up (a good idea), you would check that box on the right, for example.

In the middle section, you'll decide where to send your backup when you do it manually:

You can have it sent to your server, which is an OK place to store them, but if a hacker cracks your account, they'll wipe those out, too. It's best to download them to your computer or to have them emailed to you.

You can also schedule back-ups so that you never have to think about it. It will happen at an indicated time, automatically:

If you have backups emailed to you, don't let them build up. Save the newest version and delete the previous version. Each backup includes all the files for your blog from the first day you began posting to the current date.

CBNET PING OPTIMIZER

Remember how we discussed how WordPress "pings" blog directories every time you write a post in your blog in Chapter 5? A ping is a little informational poke to the blog directory to say, "Hey, this blog made a new post and you should go check it out and decide to where to rank it."

Pinging is an important function that you can do manually, but you can also allow WordPress to do it for you automatically by completing a setting in the "Writing" page in the "Settings" section in the left-side navigation panel.

To ping your post manually, you can use sites like "Ping-O-Matic" at http://pingomatic.com or Pingoat at http://pingoat.com . But we're busy and adding that extra step is not really what you want. You want to allow WordPress to do its job, and you want it to do the job as well as you could do it at one of the multiple pinging sites mentioned above.

To do that, all you need to do is to add these sites to the list that WordPress already started for you with http://rpc.pingomatic.com/ . Add these sites to that list:

http://rpc.weblogs.com/RPC2
http://blogsearch.google.com/ping/RPC2
http://api.feedster.com/ping
http://api.moreover.com/ping
http://api.my.yahoo.com/RPC2
http://blogdb.jp/xmlrpc
http://bulkfeeds.net/rpc
http://coreblog.org/ping/
http://ping.bitacoras.com
http://ping.bloggers.jp/rpc/
http://ping.cocolog-nifty.com/xmlrpc
http://ping.feedburner.com/
http://ping.rootblog.com/rpc.php
http://rpc.blogrolling.com/pinger/
http://topicexchange.com/RPC2
http://www.blogdigger.com/RPC2
http://www.blogpeople.net/servlet/weblogUpdates
http://xping.pubsub.com/ping/

Just copy that list and plug it in and save. Now, your pinging will be supercharged and you won't have to do another thing for it to be that way.

But there's a downside. Let's say you write a post, and publish it. Then, you realize you made a mistake or that you want to add an image to the post and forgot. When you make your changes and save the post again – WordPress will ping the services each time you do that.

Though your intentions are good, the blog directories may think that you're "ping spamming," and you really don't want that. They'll send you nasty emails and threaten to remove your blog from their service. No!

Instead, get this plugin: cbnet Ping Optimizer.

It will allow WordPress to ping, but only at selected intervals. The proper time span is not to ping within 30 minutes. So, if you have multiple authors for your blog, that's another good reason to have this plugin.

Google XML Sitemaps

I have good news and bad news. The bad news is that if we've been too "geeky" for you so far, we're about to get really geeky on you. The good news though is that you only have to do this stuff once. This plugin is going to work in the background without you ever having to think about it or touch it again. So that's the good news.

As with All-in-One SEO, XML Sitemaps is in the world of search engine optimization, and one of the most important things we want is to have our sites ranked very highly in the search engines. So when someone types, "How do I lose weight," into the search engines, hopefully, our website is going to be one of the first ones that comes at the top of Google or whatever search engine they're using.

One of the best ways help the search engines to navigate our site quickly and efficiently is by providing a sitemap, but there are two types of sitemaps. One is for the search engines – for their robots, called "spiders" that go out and search all the content on the Web in order to "index" it, and one is for humans.

For a human sitemap, think of it as a Table of Contents. So someone comes to our website and clicks on the sitemap, they can see on one page all of our categories for our website, all of our different posts, and it's organized a nice alphabetical or categorical manner.

The other type of sitemap is the one that works behind the scenes so that when a Google or Yahoo or Bing or any other search engine spider comes to our website, they can see what that site is about in a millisecond.

Google XML Sitemaps is a plugin that works just by installing and activating it. There are settings, but they're pretty complicated. Just activate the plugin and you'll be good to go. The only thing you want to do is go to your left-hand navigation panel, then "Settings/XML Sitemaps," and click the button at the top that says, "Build my sitemap."

As you learn more about search engine optimization down the road, you can always make changes and tweak how your map is build, but the parameters that they have set for you are just fine the way they are, so don't worry about it, just activate it and let it rip!

But you may be wondering why it's called "Google XML Sitemaps," and that's just because at the time of this writing, Google is the dominant search engine with more than 75% of search traffic. So, most of what search engine optimization does is geared to Google's requirements. The good news is that once you're all set for Google, you're good to go with the other search engines as well.

These are the most critical plugins for your blog. Here are some others you may want to consider:

FACEBOOK LIKE: adds a Facebook "Like" button to each of your posts so that your readers can vote your posts up in Facebook.

TWEET MEME: Works similarly to the Facebook Like button, but it allows readers to Tweet about your posts with a click of a button.

Google Analyticator: Allows you to evaluate your blog traffic in Google Analytics. (This will be explained in Chapter 14.)

SEO Slugs: Creates SEO-Friendly permalink titles for you.

Sexy Bookmarks: Adds buttons to social bookmarking sites so that readers can easily bookmark your posts.

WordPress Mobile Edition: Formats your blog posts for easier reading on a mobile phone.

Now that you have the blog set up technically as you'd like it to be, we have one more addition – one that will be the most important change toward your business success!

Chapter Seven Review

- ✓ Go into the Plugins Section of Your Blog and search for plugins.
- ✓ Activate and Configure Akismet by obtaining a WordPress API key
- ✓ Install and activate All-in-One SEO Pack and be sure to use it with every post you make.
- ✓ Install and activate WordPress Database Backup and set it to email you backups once a week.
- ✓ Install and activate cbNet Ping Optimizer
- ✓ Copy the ping list from this chapter and paste it into the bottom of Settings/Writing
- ✓ Install and activate XML Sitemaps
- ✓ Add other plugins as you desire.

Chapter Eight:

Getting Subscribers

Blogs can generate two different types of subscribers, and both are very beneficial for your business. But one group you can market to and the other, you can't. So, which group is best and how do you collect subscribers? Let's examine both groups.

First, you have the people who subscribe to your blog feed, which you may also have heard called "RSS," which is an acronym for "Really Simple Syndication." These people want to be updated whenever you make a new post. This is great because you know that people are reading and excited about your blog because they want to know about every new word you write. But, there's one drawback…

You can't market to them. In fact, you have no information about who they are at all. It's a totally anonymous subscription. You won't have their email addresses and you can't communicate them on any basis.

You can't market to an RSS subscriber. An email list subscriber is far more valuable.

A subscriber to your email list is much different. You will have access to at least the subscribers' email addresses and maybe their names, if you ask for them. You will be able to email them regularly through an autoresponder follow-up series, and you will be able to offer products in your niche to them that solve their problems.

Have you already guessed which list is more valuable?

Yes. The email subscriber list. It's a great way to offer further content to the people in your niche and to make money. So, let's talk about each of these subscriber types

RSS

As I mentioned, RSS means "Really Simple Syndication," and what makes it so amazing is that it's all plain text so it's transported through the Internet in a flash. There's no code, no images (unless you enhance your feed, which we'll also cover), and search engine spiders really love it. That's why blog posts are pretty easy to rank in search engine results, especially Google Blog search.

If you tried to read an RSS feed in your browser, it would be unintelligible. It would look like a mass of letters, all condensed and it would be very difficult. So, feed readers were invented. A feed reader allows you to read a blog feed as it was intended to be read.

Most browsers now come with feed readers as part of the browser software, but there are stand-alone feed readers, as well. Some of them are Bloglines, Feed Demon, Newz Reader, Blog Rover, AllTop, and Google Reader.

When people like what you have written in your blog, they may be interested in reading more. They'll undoubtedly subscribe to your feed. That can happen in several different ways.

The orange button with curved lines and a dot in the corner is the well-known RSS symbol:

But there are other buttons, other colors, and so on. It's smart to keep a feed subscribe button somewhere near the top of your blog. If you visit http://OvercomeEverything.com, you will see our company's blog subscribe button in the upper right-hand corner.

It's small, but that's for a reason. As we mentioned earlier, it's always better to have someone subscribe to your email list than your RSS feed. The best scenario is when people subscribe to both!

AUTORESPONDERS

You will need a way to collect and store the names and email addresses of the people who subscribe to your list. That's where a tool called an "autoresponder" comes into play. There are stand-alone software programs that you can buy to control your own mail, but I don't recommend it. Due to CAN-SPAM Act of 2003, you have to be sure that you're following the laws concerning email and an online service will help you to be in compliance.

One of the rules is that people must submit their name and email address to you and agree to be on your mailing list. This happens when people opt in, period. You don't necessarily need them to confirm that they want to do this, but it's a good rule of thumb. They do it by responding to an email sent from the autoresponder service to their inbox. This is called "double opt in," and it protects you from claims of spamming.

However, these days, it's increasingly difficult to get people to confirm their email addresses because they get so much email. Single opt in, where people fill in their name, email address, and submit it, is sufficient but will not offer the same level of protection. What you decide to offer is your decision.

In order for people to opt into your list, you need to create a "web form," which looks like this in its simplest form:

However, there are lots of different styles that work just as well.

The autoresponder we recommend is "Ninja Responder." This system allows you to easily create web forms in many different styles, will house the information for you, unsubscribe people from your list immediately (the CAN-SPAM Act requires that you honor unsubscribe requests within 10 days).

The advantages to having an online service far outweigh the benefits of having a stand-alone mail handling software. Once your list is in the thousands, tens of thousands or hundreds of thousands of people, taking care of the mailing system on your own will be overwhelming. It's obvious that having an online service will be more expensive, but in the long run, it will save you time and remember… Time IS money.

SETTING UP YOUR FIRST LIST

Each list segment that you set up at NinjaResponder is called an "autoresponder" so don't let that confuse you. To begin, sign into your account and click the link in the upper left-hand side that says, "Create and Manage Lists."

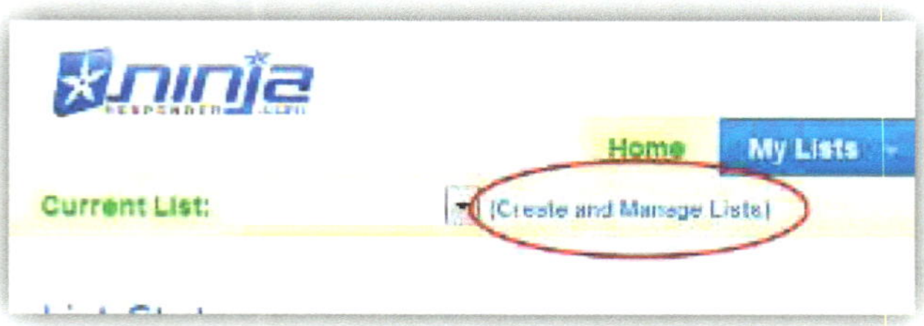

Then, you'll want to click the link at the right-side of the page that says, "Create a New List."

Then, you just start filling in the information required:

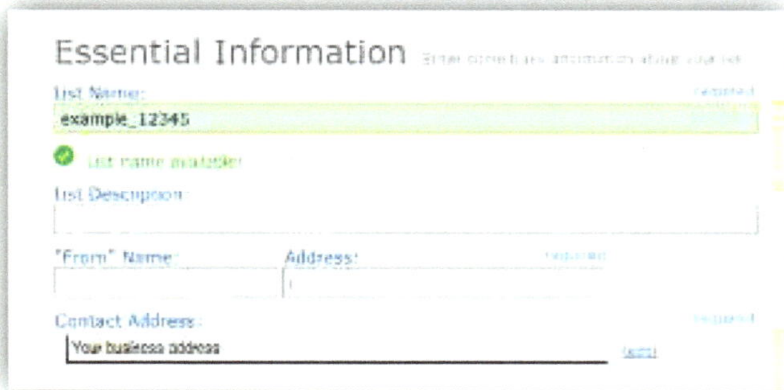

First, create a name for the list that is descriptive of what it's about. Ninjaresponder will tell you whether the label you create is available. Because each list has a separate email address. In the image above, you can see that the list name will be "example_12345." (Examples up to 1234 were taken.) The email address for this autoresponder or list will be example_12345@ninjaresponder.com. Anyone can send a blank email to this address and be added to the list.

Complete the form by adding a description of the list for your own benefit, a "from name" that will appear in the emails sent to this particular list, and an email address. You'll also want to enter your business's physical address. These two fields will be pre-populated from the data you provided when you signed up for the Ninjaresponder account, but it can easily be changed by using the "edit" function on the right side.

However, be aware that as part of the CAN-SPAM act, both a valid email address and physical address are required additions to any email that you send out.

The next section is the Business Branding Section, which you can use or leave blank:

If you are a sole proprietor of your business, you can leave the Company Name blank, but if you have a company name, that information should be completed. Also enter your website or blog URL. If you have a logo designed for your business, you would enter a URL where the image can be found.

You may want to enter an Email Signature. This might be just your name or your name and some other information. If you're selling affiliate products, you'll need a disclaimer and this would be a good place to enter that information. Here's what a disclaimer should look like this:

> "*The sender of this email receives compensation when products and services featured herein are purchased. Results are unique. Your results will vary. This is an advertisement."

By entering this copy in the email signature box and adding the variable {!signature} at the end of your emails, you will be in compliance with FTC regulations.

With that said, please be aware that I am not an attorney and would never presume to provide legal advice. Please see your attorney for all compliance and legal issues.

The next section that you will complete is the social media section:

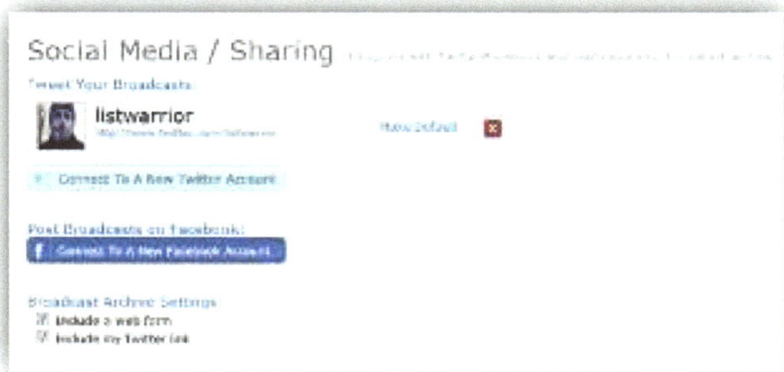

When you provide Ninjaresponder with your Twitter and Facebook login information, any broadcast messages that you send to your list will be sent to those networks. The title and a link to click will appear almost instantly in either or both of those services, and here is where you tell Ninjaresponder what you want them to do with all of your broadcasts to this list.

A broadcast message differs from a follow-up message. Follow-up messages are sent periodically to your list on a regular basis – whatever you set up. You can send them follow-up messages once a week, every few days, or even every day. In these messages you should provide great content, and now and then, offer a sales message for a product that solves a problem for the people in your niche and where you are paid an affiliate commission for doing so.

A broadcast message is any message that you sent to the list that is outside the follow-up series. You can send them as often as you like, but it's recommended that you connect with your list at least three times a week or even every day.

The last section for setting up your list is the "Notifications" section:

If you want to be notified every time someone signs up for your list, fill this information in. However, as your list grows, you'll want to stop these notifications. Your inbox will be inundated with them.

But you really don't want to be notified when someone unsubscribes from your list. If your list is small, it can be depressing! Just try to realize that it's part of the business and everyone gets them. So, leaving this part blank is probably the best way to go.

Create a Web Form for Your Blog

Now that your first list is established, it's time to build a web form for your blog. In the top menu at Ninjaresponder, go to "Web Forms."

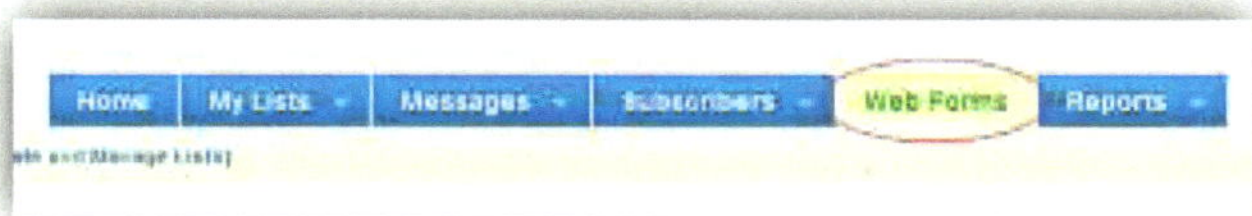

And you'll see a big green button that says, "Create Web Form." Click it.

And you'll come to a page that looks like this:

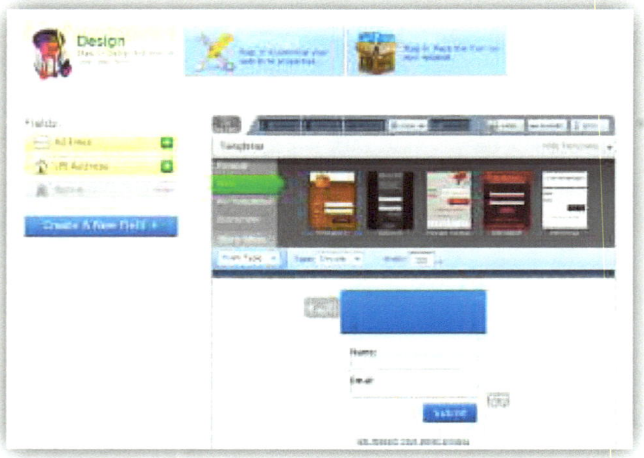

Begin with a template. Choose one that is in line with your blog design. So, for example, if your theme is black and white, you can look for a black and white template or one that has just a bit of red or blue color. Don't go nuts or it will look unprofessional.

Once you choose a template you like, you will be able to edit it even further and make it exactly as you want it. You can include more fields; however, the more you include, the less likely it is that people will complete your form. So, as only for the information you truly need.

Here's an example of how a web form template will look:

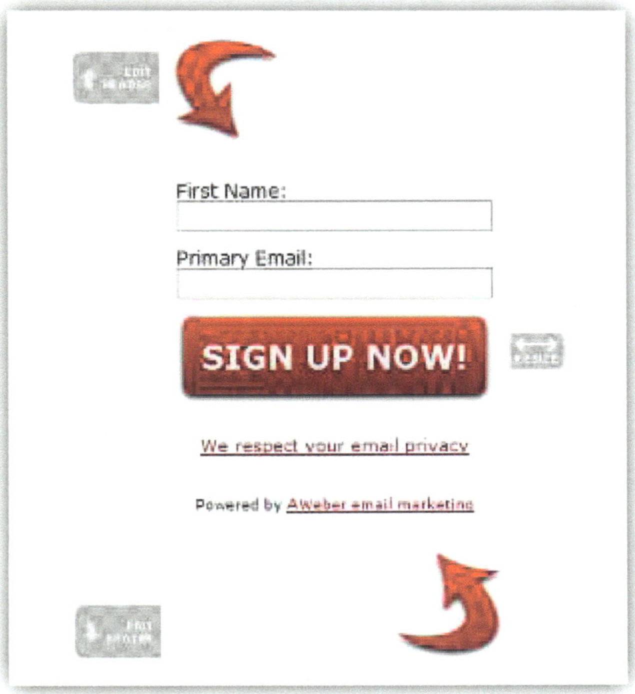

By clicking on the grey buttons, you can add copy to the header, resize the form, if need be, and edit the footer. Ninja responder/Aweber provides the links to a privacy policy, which is great. (Ninja responder is a white label of Aweber, owned by Overcome Everything, Inc.)

You can also ask for more information, such as address and telephone number; however, it's important to remember that the more information you request, the less likely it is that people will sign up for your list.

Installing the Web Form on Your Blog

Once the web form has been created, you'll need to save it and move to Step 2, which is deciding on a name for your form and where your list members will be redirected after they opt into your list.

The form name should be descriptive of where it resides. For example, since this will be on your blog, you may want to call it "blog," or if you have more than one blog, you might be more specific, as in "golfing blog" or "knitting blog."

The next option is for the thank you page. You can easily use the generic, which looks like this:

For now, that's probably sufficient, but this page is wasting valuable advertising space. When you're more proficient with creating web pages, you should change it to a custom page. Or, send people to your sales page after they opt in. You do that by choosing "custom" and inserting the URL to your sales page or an affiliate link for an affiliate product you're promoting. Just be sure that the affiliate product makes sense for the people in your niche.

Step 3 is deciding on who will install the form, and in this instance, you should select: "I will install my form" because we're going to show you how it's done.

So, after you click that button, you'll see a drop-down on the page that looks like The image on the next page.

The code for your new web form comes in two varieties. One is JavaScript and the other is Raw HTML. You should select and copy the JavaScript code. That way, you can go back to change your web form whenever you like and not have to install the

code again.

Now, go back to your blog administration area, and select "Appearance/Widgets" in the left-side navigation panel. Widgets are small bits of code that will show up in your sidebar. Some of these are pre-coded, such as Links, Categories, and Meta Data. But you can create your own. In this case, that's precisely what we're about to do.

You'll see a number of widgets available when you arrive:

You can use any of these, just by dragging them into your sidebar on the right side of that page.

You want to take a "Text" widget and drag it to the top of your sidebar.

Then, simply open the widget and paste in the code you copied for the web form. (See the image on the next page.)

Then, save and close the text widget and your form will appear on the upper right-hand side of your blog. That way, whenever someone comes to your blog, enjoys what you have written and wants more information from you, they will sign up for your list.

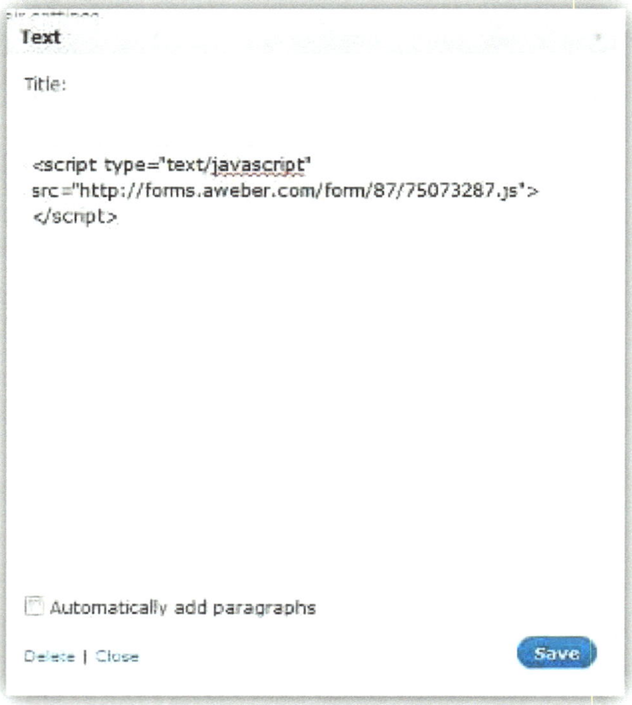

This gives you the ability to email the person anytime you like and build a relationship with them through your follow-up email series or through broadcast emails.

LIGHTBOX POP-UPS

Another very effective method of collecting names and email addresses is with a "lightbox" pop-up. You create one exactly the same way as you create an "in-line" form, except you choose "lightbox" in Step 1 instead:

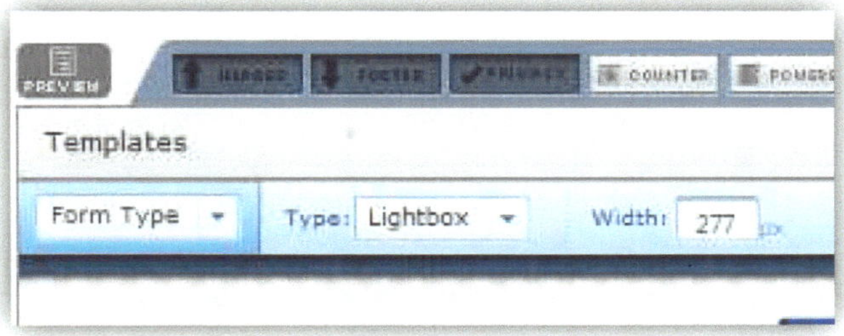

The effectiveness of lightbox pop-ups usually outweighs that of in-line forms because they come up after your reader has been on the blog page for a few seconds. The entire page darkens and your opt-in form appears. The only options if the visitor wants to continue reading is to either sign in or to close the pop-up.

All other steps in creating the web form are identical; where you place the code is different and takes a bit of tech savvy.

Because the pages of your blog are protected, the first step may be to change permissions for your "Main Index Template." Sometimes, you'll see a button at the bottom of the page, and at other times, you'll need to perform this operation in order to be able to edit. Instead of a "submit" button at the bottom of the page you want to edit, you'll see: "You need to make this file writable before you can save your changes. See the Codex for more information." You won't need to see the codex because we're going to discuss how to do this right now.

Open your blog in an FTP client, such as FireFTP, and navigate to "public_html/wp-content/ themes/ your_current_theme /index.php." Then, right click on the file, and a window will open that looks like this:

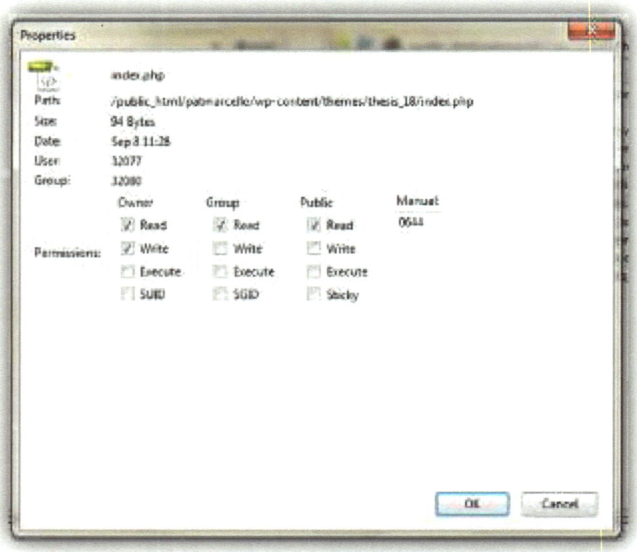

Now, you're ready to change permissions, or you may see it written, "CHMOD," which is an abbreviation for "change mode."

As you can see the permission to read in the above image is for everyone to be able to read, but not write or execute. You need to write as the blog's owner, so for you, that's permissible. But, even you can't execute, unless you CHMOD.

These are security measures to keep hackers out of your important web pages, and every page on the Web – blog or regular HTML, has permissions. They should be set to 644, unless you're editing, and then, it's OK to change them to 777, just for the short time you are editing.

Open your blog's dashboard, and then, go to Appearance/Editor. You'll see this:

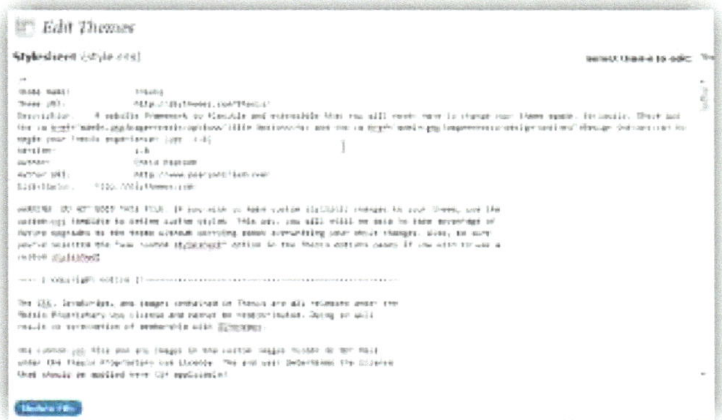

The editor always opens to your "Stylesheet," which is a .css file that tells your blog how it should look. You can change the face, size, and color of fonts here. Change your header size, and many other operations. These operations take a bit of coding knowledge that would really be for another course.

The file you want to edit is “Main Index Template, and it looks pretty much like the image above, but now, you’ll see the code for the front page of your blog. Here’s where you want the pop-up code to live.

Now, take the JavaScript code that you got from Aweber for your lightbox pop-up, and insert it at the end of the Main Index Template page, like this:

Then, click “Update File, and you should be all set.

But don’t forget! You have to CHMOD back to 644. So, just repeat the process above, or if you left your FTP program open (recommended), then, right click on index.php and change the permission to 644.

Now, every time someone visits your blog, they will see your pop-up and you will be building your list even faster!

Since we have our blog set up, let's open for business! In our next chapter, we'll talk about creating engaging posts and pages and explain the difference between them.

Chapter Eight Review

- ✓ Though RSS subscribers are good to have an email marketing list subscriber is far more valuable.
- ✓ Find a reliable autoresponder with good deliverability to manager your email marketing subscribers.
- ✓ Create a web form
- ✓ Add the form to a widget at the top of your blog's sidebar and start getting subscribers for your list!
- ✓ Optional: Add a lightbox pop-up to your blog, which is more effective.

CHAPTER NINE:

CREATING POSTS AND PAGES

The difference between posts and pages is often confusing for the new blogger. Yet, knowing which to use for what you want to convey to your readers is critical for many reasons.

First, pages never show up on the front door of your blog. So, anything that is timely or changing should be a "post." Anything that will generally remain the same is a "page." It's that simple.

HAVING THE RIGHT PAGES

Whether you realize it or not, search engine spiders have things they like to see on a blog or website and in the case of a blog, these will be your pages.

ABOUT

The "About" page should be a little bit about you. Make it conversational and appealing to readers by giving them information about yourself, in addition to what you do and what your business concerns.

For example, if you have kids, pets, hobbies, or anything you'd like to share. (Some people are leery of sharing too much information, but you really do need to give out some details so that people know you're real.) And write in the second person to make it more friendly, as if you're talking to a relative or a valued friend.

Humor is great, and if you can pull it off, it will attract more eyeballs. People love stuff that is funny. But only do it if you're sure you're good at it, or it could do more harm than good.

Frequently Asked Questions

People tend to ask the same questions over and over again, no matter what niche we're discussing. Try to come up with at least 10 questions you can answer on this blog page that will help your readers to solve problems easily.

Having the right pages in your blog is important to search engines

If you're a tad tech savvy, there is a plugin you can get that will make this page easy to construct called "FAQtastique." When you install it, it will create a place for people to ask the questions that arise as they're reading your blog posts. You can then, answer them, and create a great FAQs page on the fly.

Disclaimer

If your blog is commercial, you must have a page that explains that everyone's results will vary. Though you may have made a million dollars selling something online, that doesn't mean that everyone who buys a product from you or one of your joint venture partners will have the same results.

There are tons of disclaimer pages online, and you can probably get one from a website that generates them for you, but they may not be 100% legal or suit your purposes properly. Consult your attorney for the proper language you should be using.

Privacy Policy

A privacy policy is a must, especially if you want to use your blog to build a list. You can get one from the Better Business Bureau Online at http://www.bbbonline.org/understandingprivacy/PMRC/createpolicy.asp . But again, you should consult your attorney for total legal protection.

A privacy policy describes how you will use the information that you collect from people. Will you share it? Is it legal to share it in your state? Do you sell it? Is it legal in your state? You see, there are many considerations.

If you're keeping the information for your own business use and do not share it with anyone, that's a more straightforward approach, and one that will probably be OK with a standard privacy policy. However, I am not an attorney and don't presume to provide legal advice to you. Please consult your lawyer for the appropriate information.

Terms of Use

This document might explain how people can use your website, what will happen if they use it inappropriately, and what copyrights you provide for the material your blog houses. It can also deny liability or damage from use, as in the case of software programs. You want to outline exactly what you expect and what your customers can expect from you.

This is another document that can be drawn up by your attorney. As mentioned before, many folks simply "swipe" someone else's and adapt the document to their own business. Again, this could be dangerous. Consult your attorney for proper documentation.

A Way to Contact You

There are a couple of ways to go about this. The easiest way is to get a plugin called *WP-Contact Form.* You get a snippet of code with it that you create a page with. You title the page, insert the code into the HTML tab of a page blank, go to Settings/Contact Form and complete some basic information (what you want your thank you message to read, for example), and you're all set to go.

The cool part about this is that WP-Contact Form will send these messages to any email address you specify. So, if you have a support desk, you can have them sent straight there. Or, if you're a one-person show, set up a special mailbox in your hosting account to collect these messages. You probably won't get many to start, but once the traffic to your blog builds, you'll have some spam coming in. It's unavoidable. So, I wouldn't advise that you use your personal email address for this purpose.

The other way is just to include a page with an email address. Just don't make it "live" or you'll be spammed into oblivion! Instead, make it an image.

Create a text document that has nothing but your email address typed on it. Then, in a graphics program, crop to just the email address and save it as a .jpg file and upload that image to your hosting account. Link the image to the email address like this:

<a href="mailto:emailaddress@yourdomain.com"><img src="http://yourdomain.com/image_title.jpg"></a>

Now, when someone clicks on the link, an email blank will pop up for them and they can send you a message. Spam bots can't pick up your email address from an image, so that saves you from being spammed.

> Using an image, rather than a clickable email address, will prevent spammers from harvesting your address. Always create a .jpg image of your email address and use that in your web pages.

OTHER PAGES

Aside from the pages already mentioned, you may want to create pages for other purposes. Some themes, such as Socrates, FlexSqueeze, or The Ultimate Blogging Theme, for example, allow you to create squeeze pages and sales pages with your blog. This is great way to turn WordPress into a great affiliate marketing website!

You may also want pages that introduce readers to your affiliate products or someone else's. You can write reviews and use your affiliate links in the copy.

You can even create a sitemap for users (as opposed to the sitemaps that search bots use) or pages for any number of reasons.

WordPress makes all of this possible, and very easy. You can get plugins that will allow you to create squeeze pages, affiliate banner rotators and more. You just need to go and search for them. Some are free and some are paid, but often, the paid versions have better functionality.

CREATING POSTS

As we discussed earlier in this chapter, a post is far different from a page. Think of a post like a newspaper – filled with current events, and a page more like a book. They never change, right? So, posts are updated on your front page every time you make one, with the most recent post at the top.

This is where you'll do all the bonding with the folks in your niche. You'll tell them about things you've read, seminars you've attended, or your observations about something you've encountered when working in and studying your niche.

For example, at Overcome Everything, our entire staff contributes to the company blog. They contribute by having the feeds from their personal blogs pulled in and by writing informational posts to help our clients each week. The personal blog posts give the blog "personality," while the teaching posts help people to grow their lists and their online businesses. And because we have so many people contributing, it's a very busy blog.

Start out by writing for an hour every single day, whether you write anything or not. This habit will make it easier to fall into a routine and keep you writing with ease.

The best rule of thumb is to create your pages and allow them to exist. You may want to tweak your "About" page, for example, as things change in your life, but you probably won't even touch the rest once they're in place. But you should be creating posts every single day, especially when your blog is new. This will serve two purposes: Regular, steady posting creates subscribers. People want to know that you're going to be there giving them great information every day. They'll come to expect it of you. But unless you show consistency, your readership probably won't grow.

The other purpose this regular posting serves is to get you into the habit of writing. Most people are reluctant to write. It's hard work, if you want to write well, and we all have plenty of work to take care of in an online business. Still, this is one of the MOST important things you can to when you're just starting out. It's critical!

You need to let people know you. Who are you? What business are you in? How much do you know? Are you trustworthy? All of these questions will be answered as you continue to post regularly, and people who know, like, and trust you will buy from you.

This daily grind doesn't necessarily have to continue forever. After you have a large readership, you may want to cut your posting back a bit. Just be sure that you're posting at LEAST three times a week.

Getting Ideas

The biggest issue with most bloggers is getting ideas about what to write. But, let me make it easy for you. Sign up with Google Alerts at http://Google.com/Alerts and tell Google to notify you whenever web pages or blog posts are added to the Web with your keywords in it. That way, you'll always have information coming in that you can comment about, rewrite to your style and with your personal viewpoint, or you can even wrap articles and posts that come up on your alerts.

> Set up a Google Alert to help jump-start your brain. Google will let you know when anything in your realm of interest pops up on the Web. Set alerts for any terms that apply to your niche and if you don't want too much email, set the alert to send you a digest every week. Or, if you're determined to write every day, you may want to set the alerts to appear whenever they show up online. It's your call. Just be sure to set some alerts that will help you to create interesting blog posts for your potential and current customers.

By wrapping, I mean to add an introductory paragraph to the content, and a concluding paragraph at the bottom of the content. Just be sure to keep the original article's "byline" or author information together with it and a link back to the article or website where it came from. It's really important to give credit where credit is due, or you could be facing charges of plagiarism and asked to remove the content from your website.

OTHER MEDIA

Blog posts don't have to be written. In fact, you can use other media to convey the information you want to include in your blog.

If you're good with a camera, or even if you're a passing amateur, you can communicate with your audience via video. If you're in the dog training niche, for example, make a video about training a dog to heel with you and a dog that has learned his tricks.

You can also make Power Point presentations for video that will suffice to do the "showing" for you. Create a series of slides that helps the people in your niche to solve a problem, and record their progressive movement while you narrate over them. Simple!?

Not as easy as it might seem. Don't put all of the information you want to convey on the slide. Add some of it, but keep your

Remember to keep blog posts between 300 and 500 words in length to accommodate the Internet's short attention span.

slide interesting by adding images or graphics that will hold your audience's attention. Speak naturally as you show the slides and it will work out well.

In the absence of a video camera, you can also use audio alone. Speak into a voice recorder and "talk" your information into the blog. You can get inexpensive audio recording software. Audacity will work well for this purpose, and you can get it at http://audacity.sourceforge.net/

But if you have neither video camera not the desire or skill to speak your blog posts, what about photographs? You can also add still images to your blog and make your comments about them. I wouldn't suggest that you add the image alone. Add it, but be sure to tell a story behind it.

How to Write a Blog Post

All of the ways we described above are valid in terms of blog content, and still, the written post is the most popular form of content for blogging. So, let's talk about how a good blog post should be written first.

WRITING YOUR HEADLINE

Once you have the keyword, you need to come up with a killer headline, one that will make people sit back and notice. Getting people to read your post and not click away isn't easy, so a really solid headline is important.

Because keywords are important to search engines, it's also smart to use your main keyword first in your blog post's title.

The body of your post

After you're happy with your headline, concentrate on the body of your article. Let's assume that we're talking about a simple informational article when discussing how it should be written.

The entire piece can really be any length over 300 words. Just remember that it's hard keeping people's attention, so keeping your article shorter is better.

Start with an introductory paragraph that will tell people what your article is about. It should be about three sentences long and state your opinion or slant on the topic.

The middle of your article should go into explain your slant or topic. Again, it can be as short as three sentences, it's up to you. You can have more than one middle paragraph, if you need to go into greater detail about the topic, of course. Just remember “economy of words.” Say what you need to say and get out. People want to read quickly and move on.

The closing paragraph of your post should be a summary and a call to action. Tell readers what you want them to do when they’re finished reading and give them a link or place where they can go to do it.

Here’s an example of a very simple blog post:

A Backup Assistant Can Save Your Life!

> *Do you know what a backup assistant is? It’s a type of software that helps you to save the data stored on your computer. If you don’t have one, you’re treading on thin ice.*
>
> *Backup assistant software is inexpensive, and it can really make a difference. Imagine having a computer full of articles, videos, pictures, and all your important data that just goes down. Pffft!!! It will all be lost. With a backup assistant, you’re protected. Most software allows you to set specific intervals to backup your data automatically so you don’t even have to think about doing it yourself.*
>
> *You can use an external hard drive for backing up your files, and can get a pretty big one for under $100 these days. Or, if you don’t want to be bothered with keeping your own files backed up, try an online service, like Carbonite or Mozy. Both work very well. Just be sure you’re using something!*

> *If you're not, you're leaving yourself open for monkey business from anywhere around the world. And believe me; you really don't want this to happen to you…*
>
> *A few years ago, I woke up to the black screen of death. My computer decided to take a nosedive and just wouldn't work anymore. Everything from my hard drive was lost! Though I had some stuff backed up, it wasn't everything that I had wanted. Had I been using an online service, that would never have happened.*
>
> *These days, with the hacking and virus proliferation on the Web, you're crazy not to have a backup assistant! Losing hours of work and seeing every contact you've developed go down the drain isn't fun. Go to* http://mybackupassistant.com *and save your data and your online life today.*

Bingo!

As I mentioned, this is a pretty simple article, but it does everything we discussed above. The keyword "backup assistant" gets 33,100 searches per month, globally, and there are only 308,000 pages on the Web that contain the keyword in it.

You can hyperlink that keyword in your blog post as "anchor text," which means nothing more than a keyword that is hyperlinked. Anchor text helps search engine spiders to see what your site is about.

You'll also notice that the post is about 300 words. There are more than 3 paragraphs, but you want to leave as much "white space" in your writing as possible without making the post look too choppy. Adding some paragraph breaks makes the text look as if it's easier to read. Anything you can do to get people reading and keep them reading is highly recommended.

But the lesson here is that your posts don't have to be long and complicated, unless you want them to be. Keep them simple until you're used to writing and getting into more fulfilling posts will happen over time.

Another way to keep posting simple is by writing posts that consist of "lists." You can do the "Top 10 Websites for XYZ." Give readers a short introduction and then, the list. These are very popular to write and read because they're straightforward and easy to compile and understand.

Outsourcing Your Blog Content

If you don't have the time or the inclination to fill your blog with content, you can always pay someone else to do it for you. Here are three websites where you can find reliable ghost writers with recommendations from people they have already helped:

http://Elance.com

http://ODesk.com

http://Guru.com

There are other sites that work similarly, but these three sites have the best reputations for content creators.

You should pay between $10 and $20 for each blog post that is written for you, though you can find cheaper labor. However, when you pay less, you get less. So, if you want to spend time rewriting what you've already paid to have written, stick with authors that can command higher scales. Just don't overpay.

In the three sites mentioned above, the writers should have examples of their work. Be sure to read those over and see whether or not the style of the person's writing will be similar to your own. You want your blog to be written in a consistent "voice," and that voice should be yours.

When you find a compatible style, be sure to check the author's references. Did he or she do the work that was expected of them? Did they do it on time? What other impressions did the former employers have of the person? Was he or she professional?

Creating Video Content

The two types of video content are "live action," where someone speaks into the camera, or "screen recording," where someone shows his or her computer screen as they record the video information. Creating live action videos is easy with a Flip Video camera, which should run around $150 U. S. at the time of this writing. These cameras are about the size of a long business card. They fit in your palm and the controls are simple. It's basically point and shoot. You can use any live action video camera, of course, but the cost of more complicated models will be much higher in most cases.

To create screen recordings, you use computer software. Windows computers come equipped with Windows Live Movie Maker which will work OK, but it does have limitations.

A more robust software that is very user friendly is Camtasia Studio from TechSmith. It will allow you to add effects to the video that Movie Maker isn't capable of doing. However, the price tag is around $300.

Using a Flip Video camera is simple. Point and click and come away with a short video, perfect for the Web.

Another software that will work is called "CamStudio," and you can get it free at http://camstudio.org/. Like Windows Live Movie Maker, it has severe limitations. However, if your budget doesn't permit Camtasia, it is a free option for you to try.

Apple computers have other software to use for screen recording purposes.

Keynote is similar to Camtasia, but TechSmith does make an Apple version of their software. Any of these will work at varying degrees of sophistication.

The main thing to remember about making video is that it should be under 5 minutes for the Internet. People's attention span are short, so keeping it under 5 minutes ensures that they will watch it all the way through, or at all.

Once you have made the video, you can also upload it to one of the online video directories, like YouTube, Viddler, Daily Motion, and many more. This gets the word out, and it will help you to add the video to your blog with ease. After uploading the video to one of these sites, they provide an "embed" code that you can copy and paste into the HTML tab of your "new post" blank. That's all you need to do, if you upload your videos to one of these directories.

If you want to add the videos to your blog without adding it to YouTube or another channel, you will have to encode a "video player" for it or it will not play. You can find various player codes online, but until you're more tech savvy, you're better off letting YouTube and the other video sites do the work for you.

Adding Audio Content

As we discussed earlier, audio content is also a viable way to get information into your blog. Audacity will allow you to create an audio recording that you can easily add to your blog posts.

Either speaking into the recorder and monologuing a post or getting someone into the room with you and having a discussion are valid ways for creating an audio that your blog visitors will love.

But if you want to interview someone or discuss a topic with someone who's not in the room with you, you'll want to use a "teleconference bridge line." That way, no matter where the speakers for your audio may be located, they can call into a central line and you can use it to record your conversation.

One great service is "Free Conference Calling," at *http://FreeConferenceCalling.com* . You can have up to 500 callers, if you'd like to interview an expert and invite people from your niche to the call. The service will also record the call and create an .mp3 audio for you to download after the call has ended.

There are other free services online, but Free Conference Calling seems to be one of the best. Do some research and see which free conference calling plan might be best for you.

If you want a more sophisticated and user-friendly teleconference service, you can pay for it. One great service is our own "Safe Teleseminar," at *http://SafeTeleseminar.com* where you can schedule conferences and host replays right from the Safe Teleseminar website.

That ends our chapter on blog content. In our next chapter, we'll be talking more about search engine optimization and writing your posts with search in mind.

Chapter Nine Review

- ✓ *Create pages to help your readers. Also help increase search engine optimization rankings.*
- ✓ *Create an image from your email address to avoid spam*
- ✓ *Write in your blog every single day*
- ✓ *Compose 3-paragraph or list posts to ease the pain of writing.*
- ✓ *If you can't or don't want to write, hire a ghost writer to write for you.*
- ✓ *Add video and audio content to your blog to satisfy readers with different learning modalities.*

Chapter Ten:

Simple SEO

Search engine optimization (SEO) is something you'll need to come to terms with as an online marketer. The mere mention of those words sends some new marketers screaming into the night.

But it doesn't have to be that difficult. Some basic SEO is important, even before you begin to build your blog.

The first thing you need to do is decide how people find your site when they go to a search engine and type a search query. So, that's where we should start with choosing some great keywords that will give you some search engine status and help your blog to appear in the SERPs (search engine results pages).

Brainstorming Phase

When trying to figure out the best keywords to use, you should sit down and imagine that you don't know much about your niche but that it interests you. You're sitting in front of a blank search box, and you kind of know what you want, but you're not sure what to type into that blank to get the right results.

Take out a piece of paper or open a blank text file and write or type any words that apply to what it is you're trying to do online. In lieu of those methods, you can also use online helpers to make things come to mind.

Visual Thesaurus at http://visualthesaurus.com will open many possibilities for you. Just type a word into the search bar and a trial version will open for you. You can type in any word and get a ton of other words that you may never have considered.

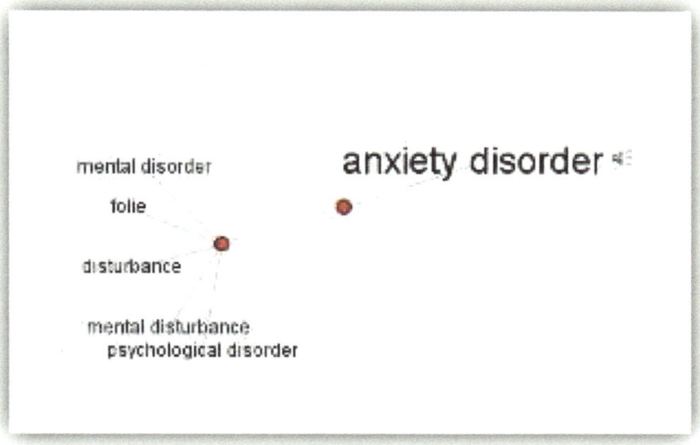

EXAMPLE 1: FROM VISUAL THESAURUS

You can also make a mind map on paper by drawing radii from your central word and branching into more and more specific terms. Software is also available to do this for free. Free Mind, which you can get at http://freemind.sourceforge.net/ . Sometimes, just having these helpers will spark your mind in directions you wouldn't normally consider.

A Concrete Example

But for this exercise, let's say you're into anxiety relief. What are some general terms that might apply?

Self-help

Anxiety

Stress relief

Insecurity

Those are very broad, aren't they? I mean, anxiety relief has lots of different tangents, but let's start with these words.

Then, take them individually, if we think of "self-help," what are some words that might apply to what you're doing. Let's say you're selling an ebook that helps people to overcome the anxiety they're feeling.

Here are some offshoots of "self-help" that would apply:

Self-help book

Self-help books for women

Self-help books for men

Self-help ebook

Self-help ebooks

Self-help for anxiety

Self-help for anxiousness

Self-help for disquiet

And so on. Just put down every word you can think of that applies to what you're trying to do.

GOOGLE'S EXTERNAL KEYWORD TOOL

Next, go to Google's External Keyword Tool at https://adwords.google.com/select/KeywordToolExternal and plug in those keywords you came up with. This tool is the most helpful because it contains statistics on what people are actually searching for on a monthly basis at Google. If we optimize our web pages for Google, the other search engines generally fall into line.

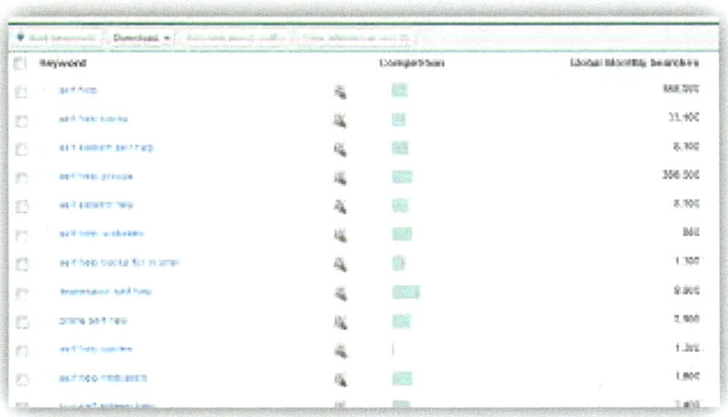

This tool will come back with about 100 examples of keywords you might be able to use, but if you open a free AdWords account, you can use the exact same tool and it will come back with hundreds more. You don't have to set up a pay-per-click

(PPC) campaign until you're ready, so it's probably a good idea to go ahead and start your account now so that it's ready when you are. Plus, you get a more powerful keyword research tool, as well.

So, let's see what comes back for the "self-help" words we came up with:

It's a little hard to see here, but you can see that just in this screen capture that there are many more keywords that will apply to what you're trying to do.

Here's the list I got:

self help

self help books

self help books for women

self help motivation

self help ebooks

self help confidence

self help advice

anxiety self help

self help books online

self help guide

self help for women

Now, if anyone was looking for self-help online, might any of these terms apply to your ebook? Probably.

But let's take the next step and do the same thing for anxiety:

anxiety

anxiety and panic attacks

anxiety panic attack symptom

anxiety panic disorder

cure anxiety and panic attacks

anxiety panic attack treatment

social anxiety disorder symptoms

generalized anxiety disorder symptoms

depression anxiety panic attacks

anxiety disorder symptoms

panic attack anxiety attack

social anxiety disorder treatment

treating anxiety and panic attack

anxiety disorder

generalized anxiety disorder

dealing with anxiety and panic attacks

social anxiety disorder

generalized anxiety disorder treatment

And a whole lot more. Any of these could apply, providing your ebook contains content on each of those topics.

The Searcher's Intent

Of course, you need to go back and put your other "general" keywords into the keyword tool, but now, you need to pick out the words that at least 3,000 searches per month, and for each appropriate keyword, try to get inside the head of your searcher.

Do they want to learn about panic attacks as associated with anxiety? If your book doesn't cover panic attacks, those words can go by the wayside.

Or, what if they're looking for a doctor to help them in their local area? If the search term is "anxiety doctor Houston," it's pretty clear that they're looking for help from a real person. Your ebook probably wouldn't satisfy their search. So, get rid of those.

Also rid your list of anything that says, "Free." Your ebook is for sale; you're not giving it away, so free doesn't apply.

WHAT'S THE COMPETITION LIKE?

Now that your list is pared down, it's time to determine how much competition you'll be up against and how powerful the sites are that they come from. For each keyword that you've chosen, you can click on its link in Google's Keyword Tool or type the keyword into a Google search box, and see how many pages exist on the Internet for that particular keyword. If you find results under 1 million, you probably have a fairly decent keyword. If it's under 500,000 pages, you have a darned good one.

You'll also want to look down the page and determine who your competitors are. If you find a keyword that has at least 3,000 searches per month, that has less than 1 million pages online, and that your customers would probably type into a search engine to find you, you're definitely on the right track.

Yet, if all of the results on the page are Wikipedia, YouTube, or other "authority" sites, you may not have a chance. Yet, if 2 to 3 of the sites on the page have rather new domains, few backlinks to the page and to the domain, and have not optimized their pages for SEO, you may have a chance to appear somewhere on the page.

This type of research takes a very long time and if you're just starting out, the first two elements are really all you need to worry about. See how many searches a keyword gets and how many pages it exists on, and if the parameters are right, you'll have some pretty good keywords when you're done.

In our next chapter, it's time to write your first search engine friendly post!

Chapter Ten Review

- ✓ Use a pencil and paper, a text file, or online software to brainstorm ideas about what you're trying to do.
- ✓ Take each keyword that you have come up with and feed it into Google's External Keyword Tool.
- ✓ Narrow the list by finding keywords that get at least 3,000 searches per month.
- ✓ Narrow the list further by trying to understand the searcher's intent.
- ✓ For each keyword you find that applies exactly to what you're trying to do, perform a Google search to see how many pages exist online for that keyword.
- ✓ Choose keywords that have under 1 million pages and you'll have some strong keywords that will work well for you.

Chapter Eleven:

How to Write a Search Friendly Post

Posting to your blog without some kind of nod to search engines is OK, if you're just a hobby blogger. But if you're in business, and want to build a list with your blog, getting the search engines involved is smart.

Search engines will give you free traffic, which is great in and of itself, but the traffic you get will also be targeted. That means they're already interested in what you're writing about, and are eager to learn what you have to share.

For example, what if someone sees your message about pet toys in a forum that is about parenting. Some of them will be interested in pets, but not many. And if they come to your site looking for dog toys when you're selling toys for cats, your message isn't going to work at all.

Yet, if they find your search engine listing about cat toys because they searched for cat toys. What's the likelihood that they'll be buyers? It's exponentially greater than a blind ad somewhere in a general medium.

So, let's start with first things first when you're preparing a search friendly blog post.

Create an SEO Friendly Title

The very first thing that search spiders look for on a web page is a title. Each post on your blog is considered to be a web page, as are each of your pages or any other page online. So, you need to make certain that every post and page in your blog has a *unique* title and description.

The worst mistake you can make when it comes to SEO is to use the same title and description on every page. So, don't be lazy and do that. Come up with a keyword for every post and use that at the **beginning** of your title.

If you use the Thesis theme, the places where you can add title and description are already there for you. But, if you're using a free theme or another paid theme, you will need to download a plugin called "All in One SEO."

This is how it looks in your blog. The cool thing about using a theme or plugin that adds this Meta data for you is that you can have a different title for the search engines than you have for your readers. If you can't easily add a keyword at the beginning of the title readers will see, that's OK. You can add one in the All in One or your theme's title and description area that is.

Here's an example of a reader-friendly title:

"Define Your Marketing Mix with Statistics"

The main keyword is: "define marketing mix." So, though that title works for blog readers, it may not be spider friendly because "your" isn't part of the main keyword.

Here's how that title should be constructed for the spiders and what you would fill into the All in One blanks:

"Define Marketing Mix with Statistics"

STAY WITHIN SET PARAMETERS

Be sure to keep your title to under 65 characters and your description to under 150 characters. Why? Because that's all that will show up for your listing in the results pages. You don't want potential visitors to have a partial title or description. You want to sell that click!

Find out how many characters are in anything you write by visiting http://www.allworldphone.com/count-words-characters.htm and plugging in the appropriate words into the second blank from the top to get your character count.

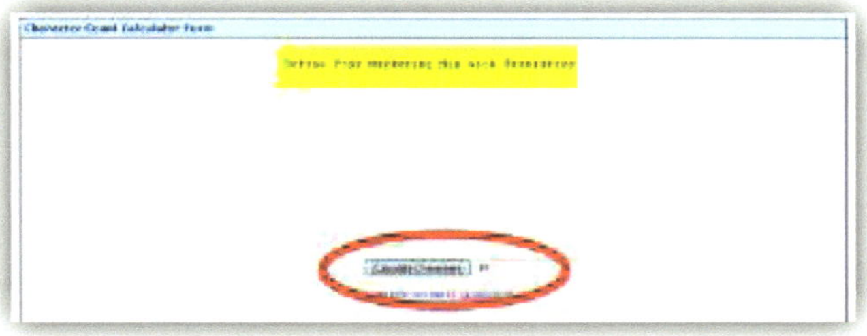

Or count them yourself. Just remember that spaces count as characters, too, as do punctuation marks.
Try not to use articles and prepositions in your SEO titles, either. These are "stop" words for search spiders. They will stop at these words and read no further. Get your keyword in first, and if you have to use stop words, make sure they appear in your title *after* the keyword you want to rank for.

SEO Friendly Descriptions

Both the SEO title and description can be created after your post is written, and there is a place for both in All in One SEO. Be sure that you use your keyword in your description as early as possible, but keep it readable. Both this SEO title and description will show up in your results page listing. You see these listings any time you search online.

Here's an example:

> Internet Marketing Tips You'll Love
> Here are some Internet marketing tips that I've learned over the years. Don't be the miner...
> http://overcomeeverything.com/1849/10-internet-marketing-tips

Can you guess what the keyword is? (A "keyword" is often a phrase.) Internet marketing tips, of course! It's first in the title, and early in the description, and if you notice, it's also part of the permanent link for that blog post's page. This is a great example of how titles and descriptions should be constructed.

KEYWORD DENSITY

Another SEO concept that you should pay attention to is "keyword density." That means, how many of the words in a piece of writing are keywords as compared to the total number of words. For example, if you wrote a 100-word post (but you should never do that. Keep posts to 300 words or more.), and 5 of those words were your keyword, you'd have a 20% keyword density, which is MUCH too high.

Try to keep your density around 2-3 percent, though the only thing you should really be concerned with is keeping your writing natural. If you can plug in the keyword as you're writing, as it comes to mind, that will usually be enough.

Search engines are pretty smart these days. You don't have to overload your post with your keyword because they can get the "gist" of what you've written with "Latent Semantic Indexing," or LSI because of the words you use that are germane to your niche. Use the keyword, but don't overdo.

Even though LSI is getting more and more powerful, you'll usually hear people telling you to use your keywords *often*. That's OK, as long as your writing remains natural. Write for your readers and keep your writing readable first before thinking of the search engines.

Duplicate content doesn't matter. You will never be penalized for it by any of the search engines. However, only one backlink for all the content you put out will be counted. Still, unique, valuable content will always be KING.

If you use too many keywords, the search engines will think that you're "keyword stuffing." You definitely don't want that because if you do it consistently, your blog will be downgraded by search engines. To check your keyword density, you can visit a free site called "Live Keyword Analysis" at http://live-keyword-analysis.com , plug your article into the blank, add up to three keywords and allow the online tool to figure the density for you.

Duplicate Content

One issue that search specialists argue about incessantly is whether or not duplicate content hurts you. What is it? Duplicate content is any piece of written content that can be found in more than one place on the web.

So, for example, let's say you put an article into Ezine Articles and then, post it to your blog. That's duplicate content. Or, you buy an article in a pack of private label rights articles and put it up on your website, as is. If 50 other people bought that same article and put it on their blogs, too – that's duplicate content.

Duplicate content won't harm you and Google won't penalize you for it, except when it's on your own website. We know this for a fact. In our ADD business, one of our websites put the same article that was on the blog on the front page of the site and into the articles section there. Though our site had been ranked #3 for ADD test, it fell to #613 overnight. We couldn't figure out what the problem was for a short while, and then realized that we had duplicate content on our own site. The instant it was removed, our site went back to its original position on the SERPs. Problem solved.

As a blogger, this also affects you. Rather than allowing a full post to appear on the front of your blog and also on the "single post page," which you get to by clicking the title link on the home page, you can shorten the post that appears on the front page, and tell readers, “read more…” or “click here to continue…”

You do that by deciding where you want the article to split. It should be about the same length every time, but definitely at a cliffhanger of a spot. Once you decide where that will be, you simple put your cursor on the spot, and click the torn paper icon:

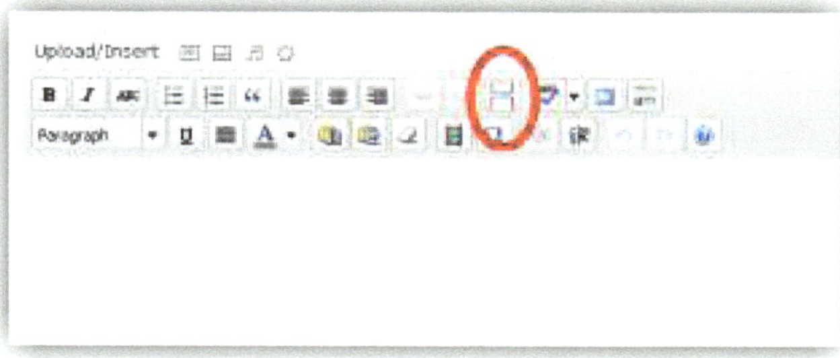

These are simple tips that can boost your blog rankings in the search results pages dramatically. Be sure to perform keyword research diligently in the beginning so that you can create a list of keywords you can write posts from them. Then, be sure to add them at the front of your title, in the body of your posts and to complete the All in One plugin area every time you post.

Keywords, Tags, and Categories

Because keywords, tags, and categories are similar, new bloggers are often confused about how to create them for your blog. Let’s get that straightened out right now.

A keyword is a word or phrase that you have researched as we described in our last chapter. These are words that you want to be seen in the search engine results pages for so that you can get organic search engine traffic.

A category is different. Think of these as classifications for your posts, and each page for each category you create should have a unique title and description. So, for example, if you're in the writing niche, where you're teaching people how to write better, you might have categories like this:

Voice

Grammar & Punctuation

Point of View

Publishing

Tips & Tricks

And each post that you write should fall into one of those categories. You can have more, of course, but remember, the more categories you create, the more work you'll need to do to make them search engine friendly.

So, if you write about how to find your writing "voice," it would go into the "Voice" category. If you write about how to write a query letter, it would go into the "Publishing" category, and so on.

Tags are similar to categories, but think of categories that people might type into a social bookmarking site to find your blog posts. So, if you wrote a post about how to interact with editors, it would go into the publishing category, but you might have tags like this:

Writing, writers, writing advice, publishing, editors

And on and on. You can use any noun that is in your blog post as a potential tag. Tags also help search engines know what your posts are about, so choose as many as you like that will get your point across.

Chapter Eleven Review

- ✓ Create an Title for your blog using the most important keyword in your list
- ✓ Create a blog description in a natural style, but be sure to use as many keywords as makes sense. Keep it to under 150 characters and be sure that it is readable.
- ✓ Keep your keyword density to between 2 and 3 percent of the total number of words in any writing.
- ✓ Create appropriate categories for your posts, and be sure to add appropriate tags to each post, as well as title and description.

CHAPTER TWELVE:

VISIT FORUMS

Becoming part of the blogging community will help you to get more traffic. Other bloggers in your niche will be eager to interact with you and if your material is good, they will link to you, helping you with your search status and in sending you traffic from their blogs.

Building a bond within your community is important. When you have support from the people in your niche, when you're recognized as a true expert, you'll have a much better chance with getting optins and a solid blog readership.

The first place you should visit is Board Tracker at http://BoardTracker.com. Here, you can search for blogs in any niche and usually come back with a decent list of blogs that you can visit, read, and where you can interact with other readers.

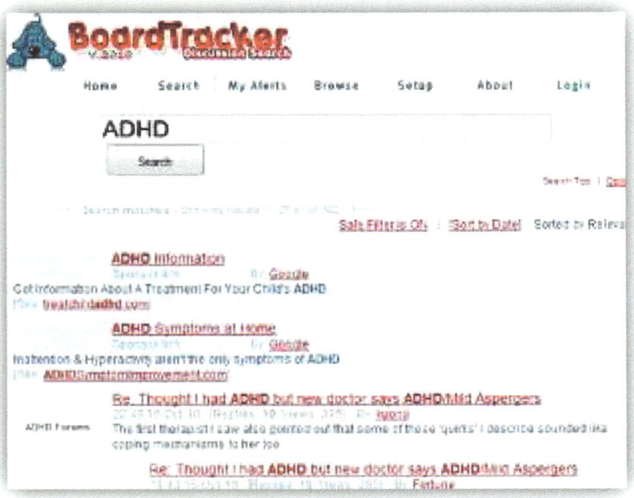

Let's say you're in the AD/HD (attention deficit hyperactivity disorder) niche. Notice the results that came up on this date on the previous page.

The first thing you'll see are sponsored sites. This means that businesses pay Board Tracker to show up at the top of those search results. It seems that Board Tracker learned this from Google as the sponsored results are exactly where they would be if this was a Google search page and the results were AdWords ads.

Under that, you'll notice the ADHD Forums, and threads of conversations that are going on there. So, it seems that the most recent topic is about ADHD and Aspberger's Syndrome. If you know a bit about what makes ADHD different from Aspberger's, you might want to respond to a post on that forum and help people to understand what those things are.

You can also see that more than 65,000 results exist for ADHD. You can look through that list, find forums that apply, become a member of each (most forums are free), and make your comments.

The cool thing about this is that if the forum allows spiders to follow your links back to your website, you're getting valuable backlinks to your site, as well.

Learn All About Blogging in Forums

Though you may be in a niche that has nothing to do with Internet marketing, you should also visit forums about blogging. Get to know the players and create relationships with them, especially if you're not terribly tech savvy.
Blogging can be as simple or as advanced as you want to make it. For example, you may want to do some custom coding to make your blog just the way you want it to be. Having bloggers that are also your friends is a great way to accomplish that.

Check Board Tracker for forums about blogging and you'll come back with plenty of forums that are about just that. But there are also forums about some of the paid themes. For example, Thesis theme has a forum at DIY.com and it's available to anyone who has purchased Thesis. There are plenty of folks in there that have learned how to customize Thesis to make it work just the way you want it to, and it can be very helpful to you.

Which Forums Are Best?

Depending on your niche, you may have any number of forums to frequent, but I'd advice sticking to one or two. Become a "regular" in each of them, and spend about 15 minutes answering questions for the people in your niche every day. This will help you to build relationships with the people in your niche and to gain authority status. The more people you help, the more your reputation will grow.

There's nothing stronger than word-of-mouth recommendations. You aren't the person telling someone how great you are or how much you know. When it comes from a third party, which makes it all the more important. Being a recognized authority in any forum will assure these types of referrals to you.

But when choosing forums to participate in, notice the frequency with which people use the forum. If it's only once a month or so, you should look for another where the traffic is higher and where you can get more exposure with a broader audience.

In addition to checking on the frequency of which people post, you can also get an idea of the forum's traffic by checking its Alexa ranking. If it's below 100,000, it probably gets a decent amount of traffic – enough to work out well for you.

Some forums may get less and be more prestigious. That's up to you to decide as someone who understands your niche.

Let's do a case study on the first forum in our Board Tracker search for blogging:

When you visit the forum, here's what you'll see:

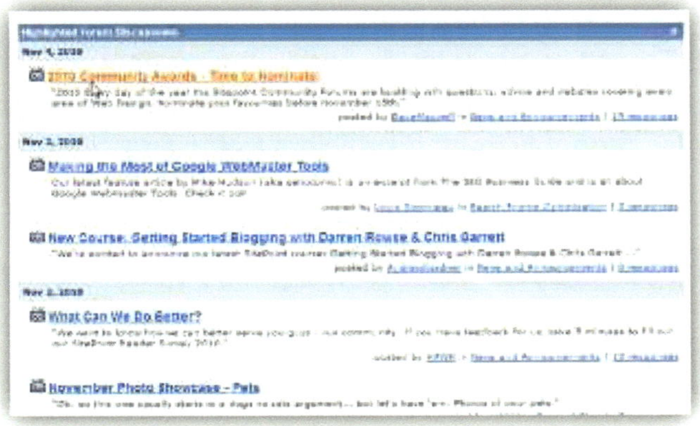

As this is November 8, you can see that the last post was made November 4. Good and recent!

Now, let's look at SitePoint.com's Alexa ranking:

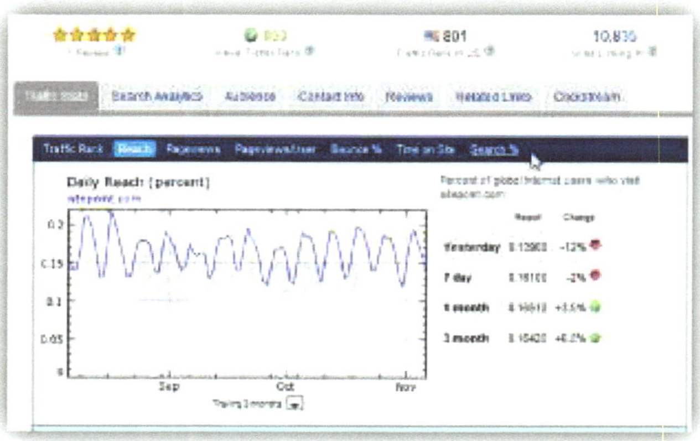

The Alexa ranking of 853 is impressive. That means that you can bet it's getting great traffic and that your postings will be seen. As I mentioned above, any sites with an Alexa under 100,000 is probably getting sufficient traffic and being involved in that forum is probably a good idea.

But see how it goes. If you're posting for a while and nobody is replying or the forum just goes dead... You may want to re-think your plan and try another forum.

Being a Valued Member

Before barging into any forum, it's a good idea to peruse the posting rules and regulations and to adhere to them lest you upset one of the regulars already in place. They can get testy and sometimes nasty and ruin what you want to achieve before you even begin.

Don't start posting immediately after reading the rule and FAQs (frequently asked questions), either. Spend some time getting to know the people in the forum. Find out who the major players are, how people communicate with them, and then, make your first post with all of the knowledge you have gained in mind.

Usually, it's best to start with an "Hello" post, one in which you tell people who you are, why you're there, and a little about you. The folks in the forum are often ready to welcome you immediately, and you'll probably notice that the same people do that all the time.

Once you get some recognition for being there, start posting some advice and some cool tips that can help people with the problems they're having in your niche. They will appreciate your help and after a time, join your list, read your blog and do all of the things that you want them to do for you.

ADVERTISING IS A BIG NO-NO, EXCEPT...

One thing you always want to avoid in a forum is blatant advertising. People really don't want to see that and if you try to do it, you'll be chastised and perhaps, ostracized. This won't help you one bit.

The only way to advertise in a forum is in a "Signature" file or "sig file." This will give people your name, and you will probably have the ability to add some anchor text to your sig file that will help you to get links back to your web page.

A sig file looks like this:

> John James
> Best Dog Training Tips

That will work well, if your main keyword is "best dog training tips." You can hyperlink that to the web page that you're interested in ranking in the search results pages.

What makes sig files so cool is that they will appear on every post you make. So, if the forum has "do follow" links, meaning they allow search spiders to follow the links back to your website and the forum has some page rank, this could be very helpful in getting all kinds of great backlinks for your site.

Most forums will allow you to have more than one line in your sig file, but don't overdo it. You might have something like this:

> John James
> My Dog Training Blog (hyperlinked to your blog)
> Follow me on Twitter (hyperlinked to your Twitter Page)
> Be my friend on Facebook (hyperlinked to your Facebook page)

Giving people multiple ways to see what you're up to is very helpful, indeed. Be sure to follow the rules of the forum, however, and keep your sig file the right length.

The only thing to realize is that forum HTML is not HTML, it's called BB Code and it looks a bit different.

Here's how you might code that "My Dog Training Blog" link:

```
[url=http://yourdomain.com]My Dog Training Blog[/url]
```

Or if you just want to place a bare link:

```
[url]http://yourdomain.com[/url]
```

(Notice that there are no spaces between the tag and the URL)

It's easy to figure out and more forums provide tutorials on how to make their sig file coding work for you.

In our next chapter, let's talk about guest blogging – what it is and how it can work out well for you.

CHAPTER TWELVE REVIEW

- ✓ Go to Board Tracker and search for forums in your niche.
- ✓ Visit the forum and see how active it is.
- ✓ Check the forum's Alexa Ranking to see if it gets enough traffic
- ✓ When you find a forum that you like, read over the FAQs and Rule and Regulations
- ✓ Spend time getting to know the people posting in the forum.
- ✓ Make an "Hello" post and allow the posters to get to know you.
- ✓ Start answering questions and building relationships with the people there

Chapter Thirteen: Guest Blogging

Blogging is a great way to build a relationship with the people in your niche. If you provide valuable content, day after day, you will be regarded as a qualified expert and people will be able to know you. That's the first step in making sales.

There are two ways to go about guest blogging. One is to write for other people's blogs, and the other is to have other bloggers write for yours. This can be a great way to broaden your base of potential customers. Plus, if you're guest blogging on authority or influential blogs, it can help your rankings in the search engines.

First, let's cover how to go about blogging for someone else.

Many of the very successful blogs online have people that guest blog for them. Some guest bloggers are regular columnists and others blog as a one-time shot. Yet, take a look at CopyBlogger for example at http://CopyBlogger.com. Most of the posts in that blog are written by authors other than Brian Clark, who owns the blog.

Yet, spots in these plum blogs are probably already taken by people who blog for it on a regular basis. So, perhaps you should try other blogs first and kind of work your way up to the more influential blogs.

Why would people write for another blog owner regularly?

Backlinks are one reason. If the blog has a high page rank, some of that "link juice" will be passed back to your blog or whatever link you choose to use in your author's bio. This will be a short explanation of who you are and why people should pay attention to what you write, like this:

> ***About the Author:* Tellman Knudson has been called "the king of list building." Get his free report** 101Ways to Build Your List ***today.***

Of course, you'll have to design your author's resource box (what this type of byline is referred to as) with regard to the number of characters allowed when submitting posts. If the blog owner isn't particular you can come up with something more elaborate, but be sure to include a call to action and a link back to your squeeze page or blog.

How to Find Blogs to Write for

Google's search function is amazing and it works for more than just websites. Google also has specialized search function, such as image search, news search, and yes, my friends… blog search.

To find it, you need only click the word "More" at the top of your Google.com search screen:

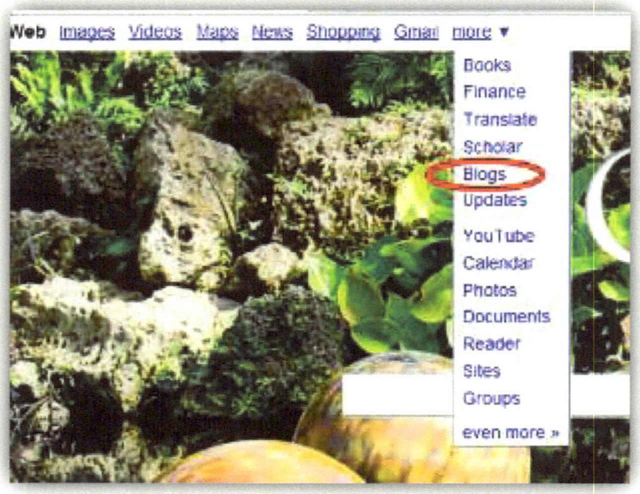

When you arrive at the Google Blog search screen, just plug in a general keyword for your niche and you'll be presented a list of blogs that you can evaluate.

Another way to find blogs in your niche is by visiting Technorati (http://technorati.com), which is the biggest and oldest blog directory online. Again, just type in a keyword for your niche to find blogs or if you want more specific blogs, type in a more specific keyword and you'll find blogs by the score.

One thing that Technorati has that Google doesn't is "authority" rankings. This can be very helpful in choosing blogs to consider guest blogging in. Of course, blogs with higher authority are optimal.

The number one blog at Technorati has an authority of 928 with most hobby bloggers having authorities of 1. Choose blogs that have Authorities somewhere in between. Also be sure to “claim” your blog at Technorati so that your blog will have greater exposure.

Blog Catalog at http://blogcatalog.com is another place to check for blogs in your niche. This is a social community for bloggers, as is My Blog Log (http://mybloglog.com). Both of these places are great for getting to know other blog owners, with whom you can build relationships and set up guest blogging arrangements, too.

Which Blogs to Choose

Of course, choosing a plum blog in your niche to guest blog on is the epitome of guest blogging, but get some of the less influential blog owners to agree to let you guest blog first. Sending a list of blogs you have written for will help your chances of guest blogging for some of the heavier hitters.

To choose a lower-echelon blog isn't difficult. The first thing to find out is how much traffic the blog is getting. If the Alexa ranking is under 100,000, that's a good rule of thumb.

You also want to be sure that the blog has page rank that is greater than your own blog's page rank. You can find out what page rank any page on the Web has by installing the Google Toolbar for Internet Explorer or Chrome. Or, if you use Firefox, get the add-on called Search Status. It will give you page rank, Alexa ranking, and other information the instant you land on the page.

Try to match the voice and style of the blog when you're writing. Otherwise, you may not have a chance.

How to Approach the Blog Owner

Before simply sending off a request to guest blog for someone, read the blog! You'd be surprised at how many people neglect to do that, and it's just plain rude. Why should you want to write for a blog you never read, anyway, right?

So, start by reading the blog for a few weeks. And, this is very important, comment on what you read. Blog owners love comments because one thing search engines love to see is interaction. This helps with search rankings and getting traffic.

Just be sure that your comments are germane to the topic of the post and that your comments aren't robotic. Those comments are liable to be deleted, rather than approved. So, don't write inane comments like, "Nice blog." Those won't help you to bond with the blog owner.

Consider what was written and add your opinion. If you can be controversial, that's good, too. Argue a point with the post writer and keep it going! Don't be antagonistic in any way; just discuss the topic as if you were having a conversation.

When Is a Good Time to Ask?

Once you have created some kind of bond with the owner, it may be time to ask. Be sure to tell the blog owner how long you've been blogging, and let them go to your blog and read some of your posts. You may even want to give him or her a list of posts that you consider to be your best writing examples. That will mean a lot.

But also be sure that your writing "tone" is similar to the style of the blog. For example, if the blog is highly technical and serious, point to posts you've made that are highly technical and serious.

If the blog is conversational, point to post of yours that are conversational in style.

Try to match the “voice” of the blog. That is very important.

If you have some good stats about how many people read these posts that might be helpful or any other information that will help to sway their decision, include those in your request, as well. What blog masters are no doubt looking for is good writing, but they also want to know that you're serious and have some kind of following. It's also an opportunity to build their lists.

How to Get People to Guest Post for You

Some of the same principles apply here. If you want someone to write for you, it should be someone who knows a great deal about your niche, and someone who blogs regularly.

It's also a good idea to see if they have a list of their own. The first clue is that they have some type of optin form on their blog, which tips you off that they're collecting names and email addresses. You never want to ask list size, unless someone volunteers that information, but the fact that they're growing a list means that they know what they're doing.

Good blogs will also have a way to contact the blogger. Sometimes it will be a contact forum, while sometimes, it will be an email link. This is one way to contact someone you're interested in, but there are other better ways to do it.

Whether you realize it or not, a HUGE part of the Internet marketing world is networking, just like it is offline. It's often a matter of who you know.

> Social marketing isn't about sending offers to your Twitter followers or your Facebook friends. It's about building relationships with the people in your niche.

Social networks are great for getting people interested in your work. You can make friends in your niche at Twitter (http://Twitter.com) or Facebook (http://FaceBook.com) and start conversations with people in your niche. You'll soon learn who the players are, and be able to get blog posts written merely because you and the blogger are friends.

But guest bloggers don't necessarily have to be bloggers, really. As long as the person who's writing has a style that is similar to yours and who knows the niche, anyone can write a guest blog. Again, if they have a list of people to send to your blog to read it (and possibly opt into your list), all the better.

If you want to, you can offer to reciprocate with a guest post on their blog. Bloggers exchange posts all the time, and it's a good way to speak to the people in a new audience that is similar to your own.

No Limits

You may be wondering how many guest posts are appropriate. The answer is as many as you want. CopyBlogger (http://copyblogger.com), for example is written almost completely by guest bloggers and Google loves the site. It's got a page rank of 6! Though Brian Clark writes in the blog often, most of his posts are written by others.

So, no amount of guest posting will hurt your blog. What the search engines and your visitors want is fresh, unique content. Whatever way you can provide that, the better off your blog will be.

When You Have a Post in Hand

So, what happens when you get a post from a guest blogger? Post is, as is. Unless there are glaring errors, like a mis-spelled title, you'll want to ask the author before making any changes. Some writers are really uptight about anyone touching their writing, so be sure to ask first.

Also be sure to keep the author's resource box intact. Don't change any links or anything about that information. It's been carefully crafted by the blogger to have maximum effect.

Be sure to hyperlink all of the blogger's links properly, as well. There's nothing worse than sending out a blog post to your list and finding out that half the links in it are dead or just not working. Fix any discrepancies in the pre-publishing stage and be sure that the links work.

You may also want to include some personalization, since it is your blog. You can write a short introduction to the post to let people know that you're not the one writing. Or, you can leave it as is with the byline under the title. Either way works.

Now that we've discussed how to get other people to blog for you, let's talk about discovering the major players in your niche.

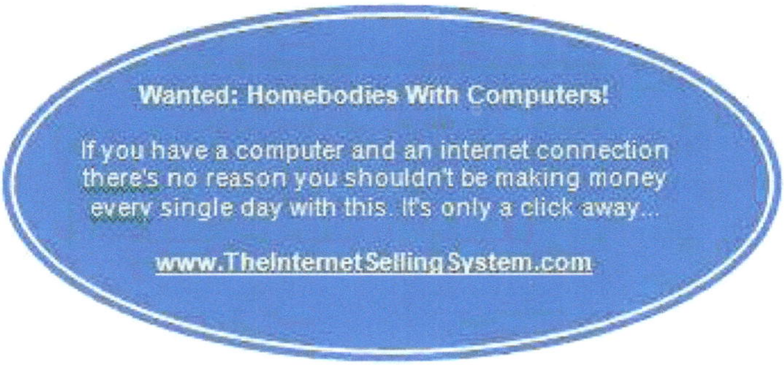

Chapter 13 Review

- ✓ Research some blogs in your niche to see if you want to write for them.
- ✓ If they're collecting optins, that's a good sign that they understand marketing.
- ✓ Try to find blogs that have higher page rank than your own or your squeeze page, if you're promoting that.
- ✓ Approach blogs you want to write for with samples of your best work and some stats about your readership (if possible)
- ✓ Study the blog's style and tone and write your post with that in mind. Try to match it in your sample article, which you will send to the blog master.
- ✓ If you want bloggers to write for you, try hanging out with them socially at Facebook or Twitter first.
- ✓ Gather as many guest posts as you wish. Google likes fresh content, regardless of where it's from. Just be sure that what you're given is unique.

CHAPTER FOURTEEN:

USING GOOGLE ANALYTICS

If you want to know how your blog is being accepted in your niche, you'll want a way to track visitors, what they visit and how often people come to your site. There are many ways you can do it but one of the most respected way is Google Analytics and using it is 100% free.

In Chapter Seven, we talked about plugins, and in that chapter I recommended that you get "Google Analyticator," but we never explained what it does.

Google Analyticator is a plugin that adds the Google Analytics code to your blog for you. All you have to do is find your UID (User ID) and plug it in.

Here's how the plugin looks after activating your account: :

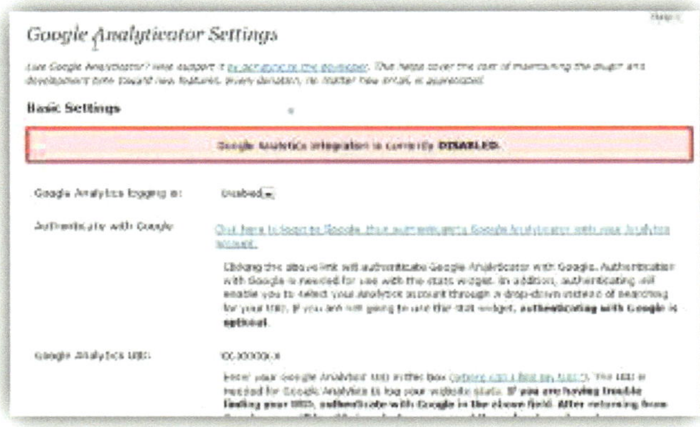

Now, you need to set up your account at Google.

Go to http://google.com/analytics and sign in with your Google ID (email and password). If you don't have a Gmail account, you can create one free and then, use your Google ID on all of Google's sites, even if you never use the Gmail address. They're great to have for business, though.

Once you have your account set up, you'll be taken to a page that looks like this:

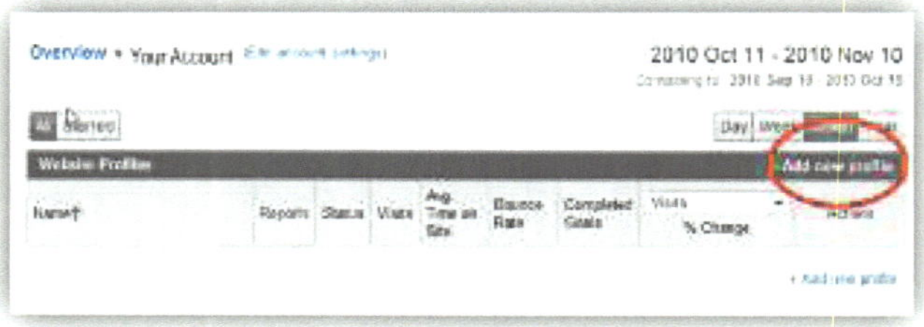

The next thing you want to do is click on "Add New Profile," which is in the upper-right corner of your page. And you'll see an image of how that looks on the next page.

Since you have a new domain, the radio button is already selected for you. All you need to do is fill in the URL. Then you'll be ready to rock. Google will ask you to put in code to track your traffic, but Analyticator does that for you, as mentioned above.

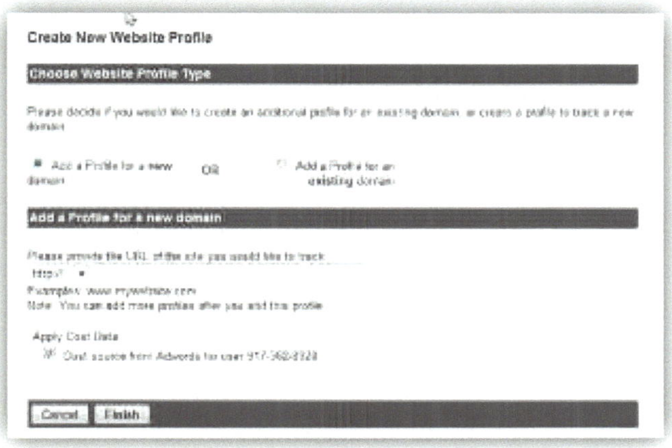

All YOU need to do is to **put your UID number into the Analyticator box and then, enable the plugin**. Here's where to find your UID:

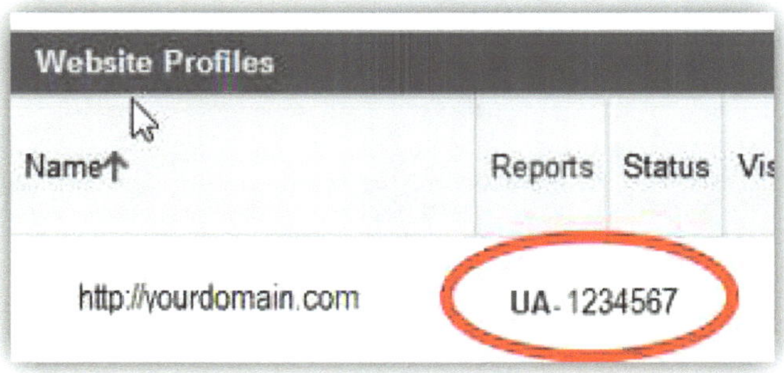

Now, take that number after UA- and feed it into the Analyticator Settings on your blog:

Get More Customers, Fans, Readers and Sales
in the Easiest Way Possible!
Watch The Video Now:
http://TheInternetSellingSystem.com

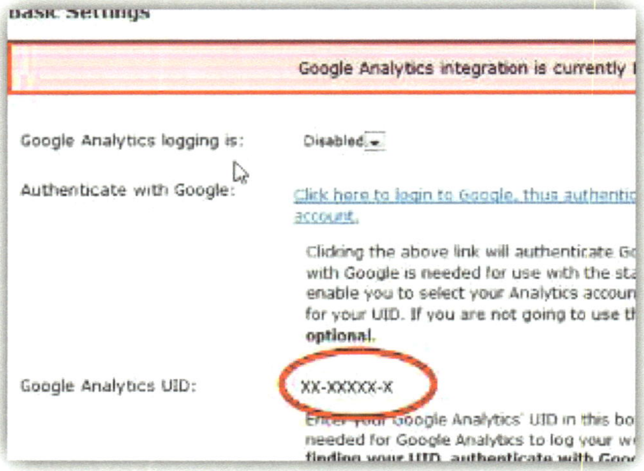

Then go back to Google and Verify your blog, by clicking "Check Status."

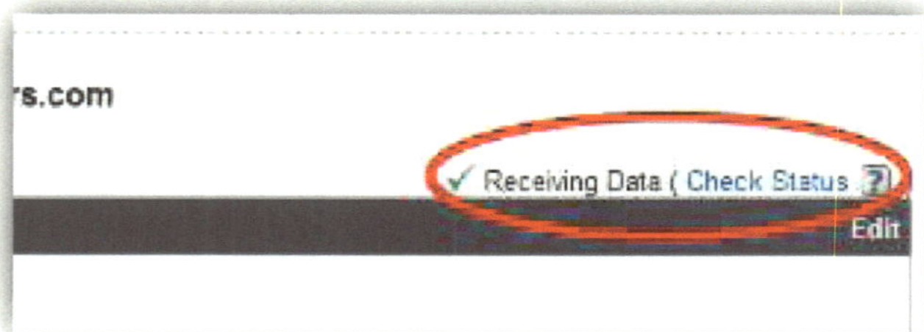

It sometimes takes a few minutes for everything to click in, but it will work for you if you follow this simple guide.

YOUR ANALYTICS DASHBOARD

Google should begin sending data from your website to Google Analytics in 24 hours. The stats that are posted are always from the day before. Here's how the dashboard of your account will look when you log in:

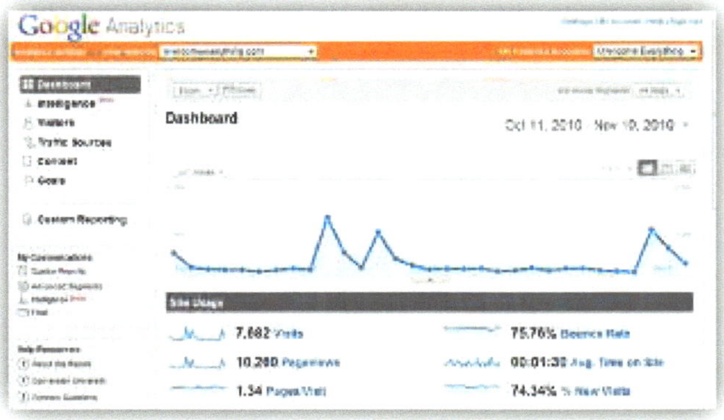

Since this is a beginner's tutorial, we won't go into the difficult statistics. Google does a great job of explaining what you'd like to know in their "Help" section, which you can get to from the upper-right corner of the page.

Some statistics you'll want to watch are your "unique visitors." These are people who are coming to your blog for the first time. It doesn't count their repeat visits, but there is a statistic that does, which we'll touch on shortly.

You also want to see how many pages of your blog people are viewing, and the "bounce rate," which means how many of them hit the page and leave right away? Also check to see what the average time that people spend on your site is.

These are all important statistics. The more people you introduce to your blog the better. The longer they stay to read your blog and how many posts they're reading will tell you if what you're writing is helpful to your audience. If it's not, they won't come back, won't spend any time on your site, and they'll just go away. So, it's important to monitor this data and to adjust your posts accordingly.

TRAFFIC SOURCES

If you click "Traffic Sources" in the left-side navigation panel, you'll see this:

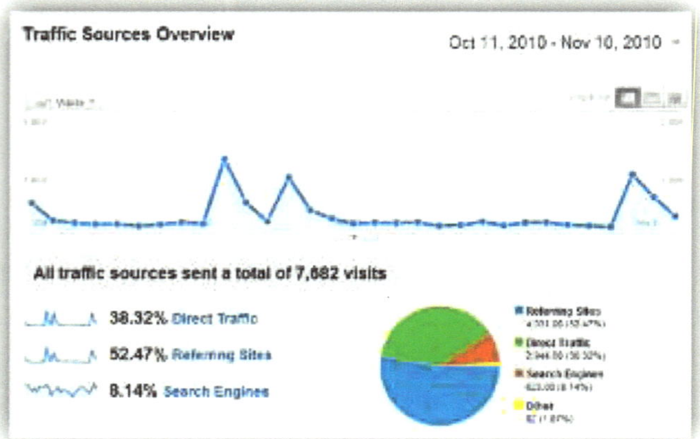

Here is where you can see where your traffic is coming from and do more of that type of traffic to boost your results. You can see how much traffic the search engines are sending to you, how many people are being referred to you, and how many people are directly typing the URL to your blog into their browser's address bars.

TOP CONTENT

If you click on "Content" in the left-side navigation panel, you can find out what your visitors are reading and what they're reading the most:

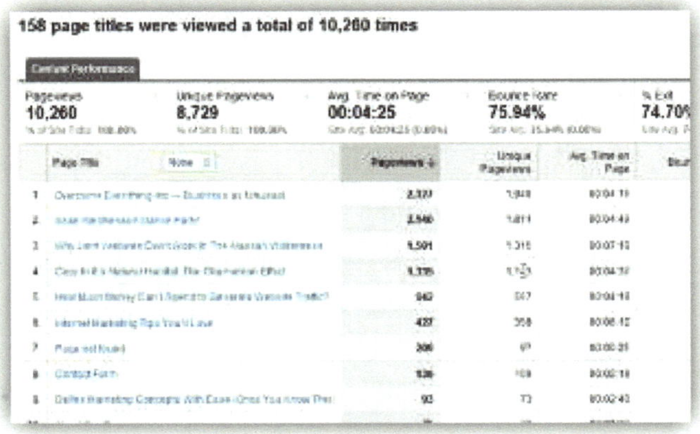

Get More Customers, Fans, Readers and Sales
in the Easiest Way Possible!
Watch The Video Now:
http://TheInternetSellingSystem.com

When you click on “Top Content” and then, “Content by Title,” you can see which posts people really vibe with and want to read. Write more posts like those and you’ll keep your readers coming back.

I’m not suggesting that you write on the same topic, but only the style of the post. For example, you may have a post that talk about a particular problem that people have in your niche. If it’s one of your popular posts, you may want to touch on that problem again and offer an alternate solution.

Knowing what your readers want is an important part of the blogging game.

In our next chapter, we’ll talk about another way to collect statistics for your blog.

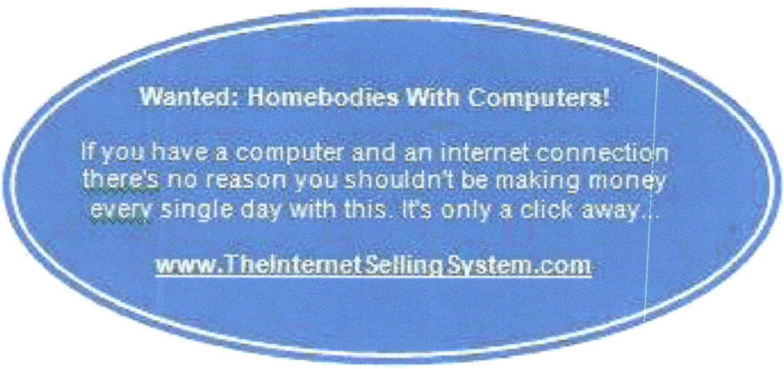

Chapter Fourteen Review

- ✓ If you haven't already, install the plugin Google Analyticator in your WordPress blog
- ✓ Sign up for your free Google Analytics account at http://google.com/analytics
- ✓ Set up a profile for your blog
- ✓ Copy the UA-XXX-XXXX number from Google
- ✓ Go back to your blog, place the UA number into the space requesting it, and enable the plugin
- ✓ When you check your stats at Google, the areas that you'll want to watch closely are "Traffic Sources," and "Top Content"

Chapter Fifteen:

Feedburner

One of the coolest sites you can join is called "Feedburner" (http://Feedburner.com) but it's not for your blog, per se… it's for your blog's RSS feed. Feedburner has many different features that you can use to make your blog feed more powerful and enticing.

As we discussed a feed is pure text, and unless you have a feed reader to read it, it will look pretty nasty. But it looks much better in a feed reader. Still, it comes across as plain text and not very appealing.

In comes Feedburner. This site, which is owned by Google now, will allow you to get stats on your blog. It will give you information about your subscribers, your visitors and allow you to add enhancements to your feed such as Google AdSense.

On the next page, you can see how Feedburner feed looks.

It's easy to read and click through to entire posts and it even gives people who aren't subscribers to subscribe through

Google Reader, Outlook, Bloglines, Yahoo, or another feed reader.

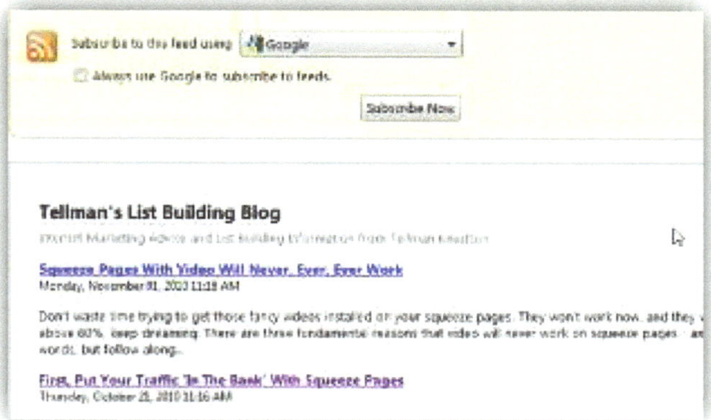

Let's take a look at the different areas of Feedburner so you can get started right away.

Burning Your Feed

The first time you log into Feedburner, you'll see this box:

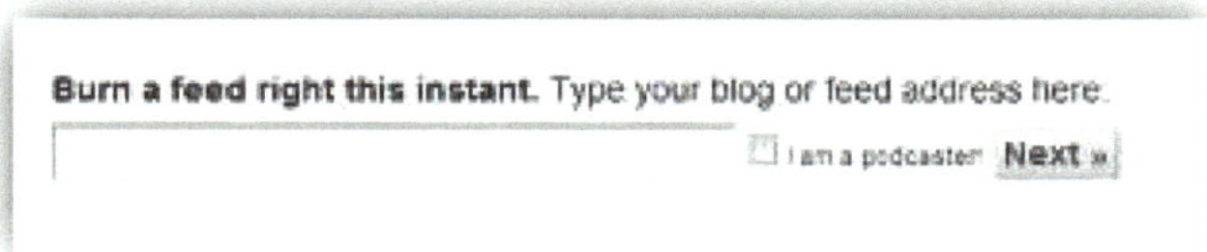

And not much else. This box will remain on your home page, but it will fall further down the page as you add more blogs. You can have as many blogs in Feedburner as you wish.

After filling in the URL to your blog's feed, you'll be almost set. To find the feed, you can go to the Meta Widget on the right-hand side of your blog and click through to your feed. The URL will be in your address bar once you arrive. The link that says "Entries RSS" is the one you want, and if you don't have this widget in your sidebar, you should drag it there, as it will allow you to log into your blog, find your feeds, and take you to WordPress.org if you need to visit there. Here's what the Meta Widget looks like once installed.

The next screen will have your Feedburner feed details and it will look similar to this:

Get More Customers, Fans, Readers and Sales
in the Easiest Way Possible!
Watch The Video Now:
http://TheInternetSellingSystem.com

The Feedburner feed address will always start with http://feeds.feedburner.com/ and then add your URL title at the end, sometimes with com and other times not. It all depends on the length of your domain.

Use your Feedburner address wherever you use your feed, such as in your blog theme. If you use Thesis or Socrates, for example, it will ask for your Feedburner feed. Some blog feed directories, such as Blog Rovver and 5z5.com. By doing this, you'll be getting statistics on usage and your subscribers will be getting an enhanced feed that they can enjoy and that will bring you more readers.

Optimizing Your Feed

When you click on the "Optimize" tab in your Feedburner account, there are some tabs you should activate to help your feed get more traffic. Here are the highlights:

- Browser Friendly: Allows your feed to be read in any Internet browser and to design how it looks. Plus, you can add a welcome message for subscribers.
- Smart Cast: Only for podcasters (those who blog with audio content alone)
- Smart Feed: Makes your feed compatible with any feed reader.

- FEED FLARE: Allows readers to bookmark your feed on social sites, to email the feed to a friend, or to add it to your Twitter and Facebook profiles.
- LINK SPLICER: Includes your Delicious, Digg, or other bookmarks as part of your feed.
- PHOTO SPLICER: Allows you to add Flickr photos to your feed.

TITLE AND DESCRIPTION BURNER: VERY important. This adds an SEO-friendly title and description to your feed.

Other optimizations include your whereabouts, adding your Amazon ID, and other activities. Those above remain the most important for you to consider.

You can also see how your feed looks to your readers at the top of the left-side column. After making changes to the appearance, it's a good idea to review them and make sure they're exactly what you want.

PUBLICIZE

This tab gives you more ways to get traffic. Here are some of the important highlights in that section:

- HEADLINE ANIMATOR: This allows you to add a banner to your website that shows your blog address and your most recent headline.

- BUZZ BOOST: This allows you to add a snippet of code that will show post from your feed anywhere you install it. It's great to use at sites like MySpace or on Facebook Pages.
- EMAIL SUBSCRIPTIONS: Add this to any web page and get email subscribers to your feed.
- PINGSHOT: Notify services when your feed updates.
- SOCIALIZE: This will also add post titles to Facebook. If you're using the "Twitter" application at Facebook, it's a good idea to let this one remain deactivated. Posting too many times to social sites is a social gaffe.

There are a few more options you can choose to use or ignore. In fact, some of the items above may not be helpful to you. You have to pick and choose to decide the best options for you.

Just remember the tools at Feedburner apply ONLY to your feed, not your blog. Though your blog generates a feed, the two are separate identities. Without Feedburner enhancements, your feed is purely information without any of the goodness.

You can also monetize your feed with Google AdSense, if you have an AdSense account. Depending on your niche, the income could be significant.

CHAPTER FIFTEEN REVIEW

- ✓ Open an account at Feedburner.com and submit or “burn” your feed.
- ✓ Choose the important options from the “Optimize” tab and activate them for your feed.
- ✓ Choose the options you’d like to employ from the “Publicize” tab and activate them for your feed.
- ✓ Add monetization from Google AdSense, if applicable and desired.

CHAPTER 16

BUILDING YOUR SQUEEZE PAGE

Now that your blog is up and running and you're getting readers to your blog, it's time to build a very important part of your system – a squeeze page.

This is a simple HTML page, usually comprised of a killer headline that will get people's attention immediately; three to five benefit-laden bullet points, so that people can see what's in it for them; and an optin box where people sign up for your list.

In this chapter, I'm going to show you how to make the squeeze page the front door to your blog or a separate page that you can use to work with your blog, even though it's independent.

HOW TO CREATE A SQUEEZE PAGE

The first thing you need to do to create a squeeze page is to get an HTML editor. Free ones are Kompozer (http://kompozer.net) and Coffee Cup (http://CoffeeCup.com), and you can use either to create your squeeze page. Dreamweaver is one of the best HTML editors you can get, but it's quite pricey. Still a great piece of software, and if you're in this for the long haul, you might want to consider it down the road.

Once you download the software, you'll want to create a new HTML document. So, just as you would in any word processing program, you type in a headline and center it on the page. Always use a red headline to get people's attention.

The size of your headline should be large. In Internet size that would be 5 or 6. Or, just choose H1 from your formatting menu.

When creating a headline, make sure that people will be immediately sucked into reading the rest of your content. Here are some headlines that you can customize for your own purposes:

"You're About To Learn 'Secrets' That Most {People/Marketers/Women/Men} Will Never Know About How To Really {What They Will Learn}..."

or

"What If SUDDENLY Realized Everything You *Thought* You Knew About {TOPIC} Was A Lie?"

or

"Who Else Wants To Learn 'Secrets' That Most {People/Marketers/Women/Men etc}Will Never Know About How To *Really* **{What They Will Learn}..."**

Bullet Points

The next part of your squeeze page is your bullet points. You should have three to five very strong benefits to outline, showing the people in your niche how your free giveaway will benefit them.

Having a giveaway or an “ethical bribe” gives people a reason to opt into your list. So, you should prepare a special report, a video, an audio, an ebook chapter, or something that you can giveaway that will help the people in your niche to solve a problem they are having.

For example, you might prepare a special report on improving putting, if you’re in the golfing niche, and your bullet points might look something like this:

- Find the perfect club that will help you to shorten your putting strokes to the hole by 50%.
- Get the perfect putting line-up to the hole so that you make the cup on your first putt, no matter where on the green your ball lands.
- Learn to size up an uneven green and make the perfect putt.

You can tell that I'm not a golfer, but can you see what a benefit is? It helps people to overcome a problem, and it always tells customers "what's in it for me."

THE OPTIN BOX

The only other requirement for your squeeze page is your optin box, which allows people to give you their names and email addresses. You've already created an optin box and installed it in your blog (Chapter 8: Getting Your First Subscriber), so you're ready to go!

Always be sure to include a privacy policy as part of your optin. If you're using NinjaResponder, then, this detail has been taken care of for you. Read through the privacy policy supplied and be sure it is true for your business.

WHERE TO HOUSE YOUR NEW SQUEEZE PAGE

The only other consideration is where to put your squeeze page. You should decide if you want people to optin to read your blog or whether you want the squeeze page to be separate.

One vote for installing the squeeze page on the front of your blog is that you're promoting your blog content as your "giveaway." Yet, the reverse side of the coin is that the blog will help you to bond with your niche, and when they've done that, they have a reason to opt in. Plus, you have a pop-up on your blog, so you'll get optins from there, anyway.

It's your decision, but I think it's best to have a separate squeeze page, to which you can drive traffic from your blog. So, people read your blog content, get value from it, and decide they want to learn more from you. If they haven't already opted in at the blog, you give them another chance to opt in to get your ethical bribe.

So, it's really up to you.

If you installed your blog in a subdirectory (/blog), it's easy to make your home or "index" page your front door. You simply install the squeeze page on the root domain and label it "index.html."

If you installed the blog on your root domain (mydomain.com), you'll either need to put the squeeze page into a subdirectory (mydomain.com/optin_page.html) or buy a new domain and adding it to your hosting account as an "add-on" domain. If your account is with HostGator and you have the Baby Gator account, you can add as many domains as you like.

Squeeze Pages as a Marketing Tool

You can use squeeze pages any way you want to, really. But you should always use them. If and when you create your own product, you should definitely use a squeeze page in front of your sales letter. It not only helps you to build your list, but makes your product seem more valuable, just because your customers have to give you their information just to see it. It's that "hidden treasure" effect that help you to sell more.

Use your new blog to send traffic to any squeeze page you like, but always, always, always be building your list. It will be your business's most valuable asset.

Imagine Owning This 99% Automatic, Fool-Proof
Step-By-Step System And Learning Secrets Like...

* An ingeniously simple secret combination that unlocks the full potential of your blogs, transforming them into automated profit pulling money machines!

* Your very first video... learn step-by-step exactly how to quickly and easily create a video presentation to promote yourself, your site or affiliate programs!

* Hate to write? Never again feel stuck, staring at a blank computer screen not knowing what to write...use these proven outsourcing secrets and resources and enjoy running your business virtually hands-free!

* Your first podcast - stepping outside of your comfort zone can actually be fun, easy and a very rewarding experience. Learn how to produce top quality audio podcasts at the push of a few buttons that excites, inspires and motivates your audience!

* How to find the right keywords that cause just the right folks to stand up, and pay attention to your offer. If you want sales, put your site in front of the right prospects. This is EASY, but most people never do it right! Here's how to use keyword magic to create rabid BUYERS!

* Facebook EXPOSED - Turns out Facebook isn't just for wasting your life away, after all. Nope, it can be one of the biggest traffic and free lead generators you'll ever use when you follow these simple steps to total Facebook domination!

* And much, much more!

Grab Your Internet Selling System NOW:
http://TheInternetSellingSystem.com

www.ingramcontent.com/pod-product-compliance
Lightning Source LLC
LaVergne TN
LVHW051128210926
848482LV00001B/14
* 9 7 8 0 6 1 5 4 5 2 1 6 6 *